# ECONOMIC CASUALTIES

# ECONOMIC CASUALTIES

## How U.S. Foreign Policy Undermines Trade, Growth, and Liberty

edited by Solveig Singleton and Daniel T. Griswold

CATO
INSTITUTE
Washington, D.C.

**Library of Congress Cataloging-in-Publication Data**

    Economic casualties : how U.S. foreign policy undermines trade,
growth and liberty / edited by Solveig Singleton and Daniel T.
Griswold.
      p.    cm.
    Includes bibliographical references and index.
    ISBN 1-882577-74-4 (cloth).— ISBN 1-882577-75-2 (pbk.)
    1. Economic sanctions, American.   2. United States—Commercial
policy.   I. Singleton, Solveig.   II. Griswold, Daniel T., 1958–   .
HF1413.5.E264   1999
337.73—dc21                                         99-17229
                                                   CIP

Printed in the United States of America.

CATO INSTITUTE
1000 Massachusetts Ave., N.W.
Washington, D.C. 20001

# Contents

# Preface

Economic sanctions have become one of the most frequently employed means of carrying out U.S. foreign policy. Sanctions are imposed to control the spread of advanced technology to terrorists or military aggressors, or to punish countries whose political systems, military activities, or human rights records are repugnant to us. Everyone agrees that democracy and human rights are good things, and that nuclear war, terrorism, and torture are bad things. The controversy about whether and when to employ economic sanctions is not about these shared values; rather, it is a disagreement about how best to match means to ends.

The essays in this book lay out the evidence that economic sanctions are not effective instruments of foreign policy, and that the economics and humanitarian costs of sanctions outweigh their benefits. The contributors draw on their expert knowledge of the potential for evading restrictions, the difficulty of reconciling restrictions with the unhampered deployment of advanced technology such as encryption and digital cash, and the impact of sanctions on U.S. business and our trading partners abroad. Their comments offer key insights into the conditions necessary for the success of economic sanctions, the wisdom of export controls, problems with money laundering laws and unilateral sanctions, and human rights issues. The papers were first presented at the Cato Institute's Global Commerce Conference, "Collateral Damage: The Economic Costs of U.S. Foreign Policy," held in Washington on June 23, 1998. The substance of Richard Cheney's paper was given as the luncheon address. The paper by Robert A. Sirico was first presented at a Cato Policy Forum on May 27, 1998. All papers have been updated for 1999.

We thank all the contributors for their hard work in preparing, updating, and editing these papers for publication. Also, special thanks to David Lampo and Elizabeth Kaplan of the Cato Institute for guiding the book through the publication process. Last but not least, we thank Ed Crane and David Boaz for their intellectual and moral guidance.

Solveig Singleton and Daniel T. Griswold

# Introduction

*Solveig Singleton and Daniel T. Griswold*

Economic sanctions are as American as apple pie—and as misguided as Prohibition. In 1807, President Thomas Jefferson confined 1,500 American ships, 20,000 seamen, and $60,000,000 worth of cargo[1] to port to starve Great Britain of the benefits of trade with the United States. Britain, at war with Napoleon, had issued an Order in Council ordering all ships to trade with French-controlled Europe only through British ports. Jefferson objected, and hoped his embargo would show Britain "that there are peaceable means of repressing injustice, by making it the interest of the aggressor to do what is just."[2] He saw the embargo as an "experiment being fully made, how far an embargo may be [an] effectual weapon in future as well as on this occasion."[3] His Secretary of the Treasury, Albert Gallatin, warned, "Governmental prohibitions do always more mischief than had been calculated; and it is not without much hesitation that a statesman should hazard to regulate the concerns of individuals as if he could do it better than themselves."[4]

Enforcing the embargo entailed harsh and unprecedented methods, leading the president's Federalist critics to call him "Thomas the First."[5] The gunboats of the United States Navy were turned against United States citizens. Shipmasters who violated the embargo faced loss of their ships and cargo and heavy fines. Customs officials were allowed to conduct searches without a warrant. Yet smuggling thrived. During the winter of 1808–09, 700 sledges carried goods between Vermont and Quebec. Jefferson declared the region of Champlain in Vermont in a state of insurrection, and considered doing the same for New York state.[6] Gallatin continued to protest, arguing that enforcing the embargo effectively would entail giving the government "dangerous and odious" powers, such as the power of dismantling all ships in port whether or not the ships intended to sail.[7]

The embargo severely damaged the U.S. economy. One merchant reported that "In 12 hours after the news of the Embargo, flour fell from 5 ½$ to 2 ½ [sic] . . . and Tobacco from 5/2 to 3$ and everything in proportion & [sic] god [sic] only knows the result."[8] In 1808, exports fell from $108 million to $22 million.[9] The revenue of the United States government shrank from $17 million to $7.8 million.[10] American merchants lost their best customers for cotton, tobacco, and flour. A sea captain wrote, "The embargo has produced dreadful effects . . . the sailors have gone off in search of employment, at least a thousand of them from New York alone, in Halifax the British have given them employment. There is . . . at this time in Philadelphia 70 thousand barrels of flour, the greatest part of which must sour."[11] The Canadian ports at Quebec City and Halifax enjoyed a boom.[12] In the end, the embargo hurt the United States far more than the British—and did nothing to end the Order in Council to which Jefferson objected.

Jefferson later protested that the embargo had forced the United States to develop its own manufacturing.[13] But this argument neglects the invisible opportunity costs of economic isolation. A new manufacturing plant is all very well, but what economic activity might have occurred instead had capital not been forcibly diverted by regulation?

The essays in this book show that little has changed since 1808.

## The Economic Cost of U.S. Foreign Policy

Economic controls are widely used as instruments of foreign policy. Insofar as sanctions and controls cannot be evaded, they deprive U.S. businesses of markets and business partners. No trade would take place if both parties did not benefit; by definition, then, every sanction that outlaws trade in certain goods and certain markets hurts U.S. citizens just as it hurts their trading partners abroad. The benefits of sanctions and controls in preserving national security are fanciful at best; and the costs are potentially enormous.

*Ted Galen Carpenter*, vice president for foreign policy at the Cato Institute, traces the growth of economic sanctions and controls to an overly ambitious U.S. foreign policy. The U.S. government routinely imposes trade sanctions in cases unconnected to any legitimate national security concern and with no prospect of success, with antinuclear sanctions against India and Pakistan among the more recent examples. "The notion that the economy should be the handmaiden to the national security state must be repudiated," he concludes.

*William H. Lash III* counts the cost of U.S. foreign policy in the loss of future opportunities for American companies. Sanctions and export controls impose initial costs in lost sales, but they also impose losses that continue for decades. The threat of sanctions and controls is clouding American business opportunities in the world's largest emerging markets, including China, Indonesia, India, Turkey, and Mexico. Foreign-owned multinational companies that otherwise would invest in the United States build facilities elsewhere to avoid U.S. export controls, thus depriving the U.S. economy of productive capital.

Halliburton Company chief executive officer and former U.S. Secretary of Defense *Dick Cheney* writes that much of the dramatic change we have seen in the last part of the 20th century has been driven by the power of ideas and that American companies have been at the heart of that process. "Our economic capabilities need to be viewed as a strategic asset in a world that is increasingly focused on economic growth and the development of market economies," he writes. While economic sanctions are appropriate in a few, well-defined circumstances, as a rule they undermine our influence, irritate our allies, and seldom work. Especially damaging have been secondary boycotts aimed at countries and firms that do business with targeted nations.

## Export Controls

Recent controversy over the export of satellite and nuclear technologies to China has focused much attention on export controls. Export controls were imposed on a grand scale during and after World War II to prevent domestic inflation by limiting exports of scarce materials such as metals, meats, cereals, building materials, and some chemicals. The controls also were intended to ensure that any exports went to the countries with greatest need.[14] Controls gained a new purpose during the cold war, to limit the transfer of military technology to eastern Europe. That justification now serves to regulate not only armaments but many types of advanced technology.

Increasingly, those technologies are "dual-use," that is, they can be used for either civilian or military purposes. Restrictions on dual-use technologies, even if intended only to restrict military applications, often have a broad economic impact on ordinary commerce. Indeed, in the case of encryption technology, export controls can restrict the use of a technology essential to the continuation of electronic commerce.

*James B. Burnham* analyzes the impact of export controls on industry and the economy as a whole. He rejects the view that recent nuclear testing in India and Pakistan justifies strengthening export controls, as such controls, particularly if imposed unilaterally, have only a trivial impact on nuclear proliferation. He concludes with six general principles that lawmakers considering export controls should follow, the first of which is that the export of goods, services, and data by private parties should be viewed as normal commercial activity, not a special privilege granted by government.

*William A. Reinsch*, undersecretary for Export Administration for the Department of Commerce, describes recent adaptations to export control policies with a focus on nuclear proliferation controls. He points out that it is fruitless to try to control items available from many different countries around the world. A second factor is that the United States desires an ongoing "dialogue" with many of the countries that are targets of technology controls, suggesting that controls should be narrowly targeted against their weapons control programs and little else. A third factor is that there is little consensus as to what countries should be targeted by export controls.

*R. Ian Butterfield* writes of the impact of export controls on the nuclear industry. He first notes that the inconsistent and too-frequent use of trade sanctions recently suggests they have become "not so much a foreign policy tool as an expression of national pique." U.S. companies have been barred from serving the enormous demand for nuclear energy in China by export controls, though there is no connection between civilian light-water nuclear plants and nuclear weapons. No other nuclear supplier nation refused to serve the Chinese demand. And China already has nuclear weapons. He concludes that the U.S. nuclear industry should be allowed to compete in the international market on the same terms as its international rivals.

A primary reason that export controls remain a popular tool of foreign policy despite their lack of efficacy is our stubborn refusal to accept that there are no good alternatives to accepting the drawbacks of free trade along with the enormous benefits. Leading cryptographer *Carl Ellison* explores one alternative to encryption export controls, commonly termed "Government Access to Keys" or GAK. Those worried that terrorists will use encryption to hide from national security forces have argued that encryption could be freely exported if the government were guaranteed access to the decrypted content of encrypted messages. Ellison points out that the costs of both encryption export controls and the proposed GAK alternative far outweigh the speculative benefits.

## Flow-of-Capital Controls

In 1986, Congress passed the Money Laundering Control Act. The law was aimed at drug kingpins, but requires banks to report *anyone* who exchanges more than a few thousand dollars in cash. The Constitution's Fourth Amendment protects our privacy by stipulating warrants to conduct a search may be issued only for probable cause. Money laundering laws violate the Fourth Amendment's privacy protections by giving the government access to our financial records when there is only the remotest chance that the reported transaction is criminal. Thus far, the courts have failed to recognize this.

Also, the money laundering laws entail substantial penalties for mere paperwork violations. Perhaps the tide is now turning. In June 1998, Justice Clarence Thomas declared in *United States v. Bajakajian* [15] that Hosep Bajakajian's failure to fill out a form reporting that he was taking $357,144 out of the country to repay a legal debt could not constitutionally be punished by the confiscation of the entire amount. The Court found that "full forfeiture of respondent's currency would be grossly disproportional to the gravity of his offense."[16] Just as in the recent Supreme Court case, America's money laundering laws impose a burden on the U.S. economy far out of proportion to any foreign policy objective.

In his essay, *Richard W. Rahn* describes how money laundering laws entail attempts to impose U.S. law on other countries. Many countries require banks to protect their customer's privacy and protect pseudononymous accounts, while U.S. law demands the opposite, putting international banks in the difficult situation of trying to comply with incompatible laws. Rahn also points out how the laws fail cost-benefit analysis. The laws impose millions of dollars in paperwork costs on U.S. banks that are passed on to bank customers, yet have little or no impact on organized crime.

The development of digital cash will make money laundering laws difficult to enforce. Digital cash is money in digital form, a means of payment that can be transmitted instantaneously anywhere in the world. Like paper cash, digital cash systems can be essentially anonymous and create no audit trail. *Eric Hughes*, a leading developer of security systems for electronic commerce, describes how suppressing the development of digital cash to preserve money laundering law will prevent businesses from developing an infrastructure to handle some of the security problems raised by digital cash.

## Trade Sanctions

The United States often acts alone or nearly alone in outlawing trade with certain countries or in certain commodities. Attempting to affect the behavior of a foreign government by this means is futile. Why do we persist in the face of obvious failure? Perhaps the answer is extraordinary arrogance; the architects of America's unilateral trade sanctions policy may not believe that other countries can supply alternatives for U.S. commodities. More likely, however, is that unilateral sanctions are maintained because U.S. policymakers sincerely believe that sanctions have value as a symbolic gesture or that they are "doing the right thing" even though it may be ineffectual. These essays suggest that any such value is far outweighed by the costs.

*Ambassador Clayton Yeutter,* former U.S. Trade Representative and Secretary of Agriculture, writes that we have not learned the lessons of 25 years of failed sanctions dating back to the soybean embargo of 1974. American farmers are still paying the price for that mistake and other attempts to use food as a weapon of foreign policy. By disrupting long-term business relationships, sanctions punish American companies for years after they are imposed. A more effective and less costly U.S. foreign policy would emphasize diplomatic pressure and multilateral cooperation.

*Gary Clyde Hufbauer,* senior fellow at the Institute for International Economics, recounts the history of America's use of sanctions to achieve foreign policy goals, beginning with Woodrow Wilson's idealistic belief that "a nation boycotted is a nation that is in sight of surrender." Wilson was simply wrong, Hufbauer contends. Most sanctions imposed this century have failed to achieve their objectives. They hurt the most vulnerable in the target countries—the poor, the very young, the sick—while strengthening the political, military, and economic elites. To minimize unintended damage, sanctions should be multilateral, flexible, and narrowly targeted.

*William C. Lane*, the Washington director of government affairs for Caterpillar Inc., describes the effort by U.S. companies to turn the political tide against the use of sanctions. Coalitions such as USA\*ENGAGE, a group of 676 companies, have tried to educate Congress on the damaging effects U.S. foreign policy has inflicted on American business. Sanctions have tagged U.S. firms as "unreliable suppliers" in the international marketplace while ceding markets to foreign competitors, who are then able to reap the benefits of increasing economies of scale. A more rational U.S. policy will require legislative restraints that will force more careful consideration before future sanctions are imposed.

## Human Rights and Civil Wrongs

The premise of some sanctions is that barring trade with a foreign country will stop that country's government from violating human rights. But foreign governments rarely, if ever, bear the brunt of the economic injury themselves, and so rarely, if ever, respond as hoped. Both U.S. citizens and those of other countries want to trade with one another despite the sanctions and are motivated to evade the restrictions, legally or otherwise. Those responsible for enforcing the laws thus must call for more and more draconian powers. Ultimately, virtually all of the costs of economic sanctions are borne by people innocent of any role in the targeted country's weapons or human rights policy. Sanctions violate the rights of free citizens to trade with one another, do nothing to erode the power of foreign police states, and seem only to encourage the growth of police power here. The mystery, then, is not why anyone could support free trade with an oppressive nation—but how anyone could support sanctions as an instrument of human rights.

*The Rev. Robert A. Sirico*, president of the Acton Institute for the Study of Religion and Liberty, argues for a foreign policy that combines "moral passion and economic understanding." He calls on politically active Christians to acknowledge that America's policy of engagement has helped to promote higher living standards and greater respect for human rights in China. At the same time, he urges U.S. multinational companies to talk about human rights abuses and to be consistent in their calls for free trade by opposing federally funded export and investment subsidies.

Export controls have been pressed on universities engaged in basic technology research. Attempts to restrict the publication of academic research or what a professor may say in his or her classroom raise obvious and immediate First Amendment issues. Attorney *Kenneth C. Bass* addresses the ways that encryption export controls violate our First Amendment rights. He points out that export controls affect not only academics who wish to publish research on cryptography, but any citizen who wants to use encryption to communicate.

## Terms of Engagement

Three important themes emerge from the essays in this book.

The first is that current U.S. foreign policy is compromising the nation's engagement in the global economy. The Cato Institute and other critics of U.S. foreign policy have often been tagged with the label of "isolationist." The label certainly does not fit the message of this book, which is a sustained argument for engagement in global trade, investment, and communications. In contrast, the controls and sanctions criticized here represent disengagement by a thousand cuts.

A realistic foreign policy would recognize the power of American civil society—and the limitations of government—to influence the world in our favor. When American companies invest abroad, they take with them American values such as individual liberty, the rule of law, and the right to property. When we export goods and services, we also export ideas, culture, and a general way of thinking about the world. The same open door that allows the sale of software, supercomputers, and nuclear-power technology also allows American tourists, missionaries, and academics to pass through. The cumulative effect of export controls, money laundering laws, and trade sanctions is to isolate Americans incrementally from people in other countries.

A second theme is that sanctions and controls are not "foreign policy on the cheap." Quite the contrary. Americans are paying a high price every day for U.S. foreign policy through opportunity costs, economic inefficiencies, and diminished civil liberties. The most obvious cost imposed is lost export opportunities, estimated to be $15 billion to $19 billion a year. Other costs are less visible and immediate, but just as real and substantial. Sanctions and controls damage future sales by tagging U.S. companies as unreliable suppliers. They hurt American companies in emerging markets where potential sales growth is greatest. They can impose lasting damage on entire sectors of the U.S. economy by forfeiting export markets to foreign competition. They impose huge paperwork costs, especially on financial institutions, and encourage unproductive lobbying and rent seeking.

U.S. foreign policy has chilled technological progress and free speech. Controls on encryption software threaten to retard development of this important technology and potentially to stunt the growth of electronic commerce on the Internet. Those same controls have compromised the ability of Americans to protect their privacy from government intrusion. The whole language of mathematics has been exposed to government monitoring because of its inseparable link to encryption development. For the sake of misguided foreign policy goals, a book stored on a floppy disk is not accorded the same First Amendment protections as one printed on paper. In a mistaken effort to advance American interests abroad, we are undermining American principles at home.

A final major theme of *Economic Casualties* is that current U.S. foreign policy fails even under its own terms. Along with undermining growth, trade, and liberty, the controls and sanctions criticized in this book are undermining our nation's strategic interests in the world. The most obvious example of counterproductive foreign policy is the use of sanctions. They almost always fail to achieve their stated objectives. Instead, sanctions diminish American engagement and influence in the targeted country, while strengthening the hand of the very rulers we are trying to undermine. Secondary boycotts such as those aimed at nations and firms that trade with Cuba, Iran, and Libya serve only to estrange the United States from its natural allies. Export controls on encryption software blunt America's technological edge in the global economy and compromise one of our principal assets.

Current makers of U.S. foreign policy do not appreciate the beneficial influence of American commercial engagement. In 1997, Americans bought and sold more than $2 trillion worth of goods and services in the global economy. American citizens own more than $5.0 trillion in assets in foreign countries, and foreigners own more than $6.3 trillion in assets in the United States. American multinational companies are establishing a growing presence in virtually every country where they are allowed. American products, culture, language, and ideas, along with Americans themselves, are permeating just about every corner of the world save a few self-isolated outposts. This growing engagement is changing the United States, but it is also changing the world. U.S. foreign policy is undermining the positive influence this engagement of U.S. civil society is having on the rest of the world. Instead, in a mistaken and counterproductive effort to punish regimes that have fallen out of favor, our own government seeks to diminish Americans' engagement in global commerce—and hence our nation's global influence.

*Economic Casualties: How U.S. Foreign Policy Undermines Trade, Growth, and Liberty* is a call not for isolation but for unflinching engagement in the global economy. If the people of the United States are allowed by their government to trade, invest, and communicate freely with people in the rest of the world, the only casualties will be tyranny, poverty, and ignorance.

## Notes

1. Garrett Ward Sheldon, *The Political Philosophy of Thomas Jefferson* (Baltimore: The Johns Hopkins University Press, 1991), p. 100.

2. Thomas Jefferson to William M. Cabell, June 29, 1807, quoted in Andrew A. Lipscomb and Albert Ellery Bergh, eds., *The Writings of Thomas Jefferson*, 20 vols. (Washington: Thomas Jefferson Memorial Association, 1904–05), ix, p. 53.

3. Jefferson to Albert Gallatin, ibid. at xiv, p. 428.

4. Gallatin to Jefferson, quoted in Nathan Schachner, *Thomas Jefferson: A Biography* (London: Thomas Yoseloff, 1951), p. 860.

5. Sheldon, p. 100.

6. Schachner, p. 871.

7. Gallatin, quoted in Schachner, p. 872.

8. John Kelly, quoted in Schachner, p. 863.

9. John C. Miller, *Toward a More Perfect Union: The American Republic 1783–1815* (Glenview, Illinois: Scott, Foresman & Company, 1970), p. 215.

10. Ibid.

11. Journal of a Captain Henry Massey, quoted in Schachner, p. 866.

12. Miller, pp. 214–17.

13. Doron S. Ben-Atar, *The Origins of Jeffersonian Commercial Policy and Diplomacy* (New York: St. Martin's Press, 1993), p. 167.

14. Committee on Banking and Currency, "Senate Report No. 31: Export Control Act of 1949," 81st Congress, First Session, U.S. Code Congressional Service, 1949, pp. 1094, 1096.

15. 1998 U.S. Lexis 4172, 118 S. Ct. 2028 (1998).

16. Ibid. at 35.

PART I


OVERVIEW: THE ECONOMIC COST OF
U.S. FOREIGN POLICY

# 1. Eagle in the China Shop: The Economic Consequences of U.S. Global Meddling

*Ted Galen Carpenter*

Proponents of Washington's global interventionist foreign policy are fond of citing a litany of alleged benefits. America's leadership role, they contend, has not only reduced the danger of aggression by predatory states, it has created a stable arena for international trade and investment. Such an environment provided an economic bonanza for the free world during the cold war, and with the demise of the Soviet empire, similar blessings are now available to an even larger portion of the globe. Although all nations willing to participate in the global economy benefit from the pax Americana, goes the argument, American corporations and citizens ultimately benefit the most because of the unparalleled size and efficiency of the U.S. economy.

That thesis contains some truth. Although advocates of the status quo exaggerate mightily when they contend that the only alternative to continued U.S. hegemony would be global chaos, there is little doubt that Washington's dominant role has helped produce a stable international system conducive to trade and investment. Nevertheless, analyses that focus on the benefits of pax Americana while evading any discussion of the costs are incomplete and misleading. The economic costs alone, paid by the American people, to maintain Washington's hegemonic policy have been substantial and pervasive.[1]

For example, the demands of that role require a large and expensive military establishment. Despite the end of the cold war, U.S. military spending (currently at $270 billion per year) dwarfs that of

Ted Galen Carpenter is vice president for defense and foreign policy studies at the Cato Institute.

other industrialized countries. Japan spends just $42 billion and Germany a mere $27 billion. Each American must pay more than $1,000 a year to support the military; the burden for each German or Japanese is about $320. The opportunity cost to American taxpayers—and to the American economy—is considerable, and has been for many decades.[2] That huge disparity in military spending is just one tangible example of the financial price tag of sustaining a foreign policy based on maintaining U.S. global leadership and responsibility.

The economic impact goes far beyond the burden of excessive military spending—or the additional billions of dollars spent each year on foreign aid programs motivated in large part by a desire to buy influence. Early in the 20th century, social critic Randolph Bourne observed that "war is the health of the state," by which he meant that governmental power inexorably expands at the expense of individual freedom during periods of armed conflict. Robert Higgs's seminal book, *Crisis and Leviathan,* later documented that observation, showing how many of the tax and regulatory powers now routinely exercised by the federal government were not acquired during such spasms of domestic "reform" as the Progressive Era, the New Deal, and the Great Society. Instead, they emerged because of national mobilizations to fight the two world wars. Moreover, the New Deal and the Great Society were explicit attempts to replicate in peacetime the mobilization of human talent and natural resources that had previously occurred during wartime.[3]

Even when the nation terminated its war mobilizations, a sizable residue of enhanced governmental power always remained. Manifestations of that "wartime" authority would later surface during peacetime—often in unexpected, if not bizarre, ways. For example, President Richard Nixon based his 1971 executive order imposing wage and price controls on an obscure provision of the Trading with the Enemy Act of 1917, enacted during the early days of World War I but still in effect more than five decades later.

The residue of wartime powers has been an important factor in the long-term expansion of the size and scope of the political state. One "temporary" measure enacted during World War II was the withholding provision of the federal income tax. That device has the insidious effect of disguising the magnitude of the true burden on most American taxpayers by "painlessly" extracting the money from their paychecks before they get an opportunity to see (and use) those funds. For such taxpayers, the category of gross salary or wages is little more than a meaningless bookkeeping entry on their payroll check stubs. One suspects that citizens would be decidedly less passive about today's bloated tax burden if they had to experience the pain of writing annual or quarterly checks to the Internal Revenue Service. A wartime innovation has thus become an important, permanent building block of oversized government.

Bourne's observation about war being the health of the state is correct but incomplete. A full-blown war is not the only thing that leads to economic regimentation and other abuses. An atmosphere of perpetual crisis and preparation for possible conflict can produce a similar result. The creation of a national security state to wage the cold war resulted in many of the same domestic problems and distortions that had been associated with earlier periods of actual combat. America has been essentially on a war footing for more than half a century, and the result is a significant erosion of economic liberty. Moreover, the end of the cold war has not brought a retrenchment in either the nation's global role or the national security state.

Even more troubling, Americans have come to passively accept governmental economic intrusions in the name of "national security" that they would have ferociously opposed in earlier eras. Politicians learned that the easiest way to overcome opposition to schemes to expand their power was to portray initiatives as necessary for the security of the nation. Sometimes such rationales have been exceedingly strained. The statute that first involved the federal government in elementary and secondary education, for example, was the National Defense Education Act. Similarly, the legislation funding the interstate highway system was the National Defense Highway Act. In retrospect, it is surprising that the sponsors of Medicare did not fashion their bill as the "National Defense Elderly Care Act."

Government also guides (if not dominates) the American economy in the name of national security, much as it would during a wartime mobilization. The emergence of multibillion-dollar firms whose principal (and in some cases sole) customer is the Pentagon is testimony to that development. There are also widespread restraints on foreign commerce for the explicit purpose of advancing Washington's foreign policy agenda. Trade embargoes are imposed routinely on countries that are out of favor with the United States. In addition to

5

such sanctions, there exist a variety of restrictions on the export of technologies that the government decides (often arbitrarily) could have military applications or other national security implications.

Perhaps most disturbing, many of those intrusions have increased rather than decreased (contrary to initial expectations) since the end of the cold war. For example, President Clinton's Export Council reports that the United States has various economic sanctions in effect against 70 countries.[4] Yet even that total apparently does not satisfy hard-core advocates of "sending a message" to foreign countries through economic coercion. According to a report issued in early June 1998 by the National Association of Manufacturers, Congress is considering 26 separate new sanctions measures aimed at 10 countries. That list does not include 11 other proposals, so-called generic sanctions, which would target any country that engages in specific conduct deemed unacceptable by Congress. The proscribed offenses include such things as failing to combat corruption or showing a "hostile" attitude toward American business.[5] The increasing fondness for imposing sanctions makes American overseas trade and investment hostage to the whims and parochial agendas of either Congress or the Executive branch.

Countries as diverse as Iran, Cuba, Serbia, Colombia, Burma, and India have already felt Washington's economic lash for transgressions, real or imagined. Sometimes the initiatives have come from the Executive branch, but increasingly they are the result of congressional pressure or outright legislative mandates. Sanctions are being imposed for a bewildering array of motives and policy goals, most of which have little, if anything, to do with protecting national security—the ostensible justification. Instead, they have become the default option for political and moral posturing. There are tangible victims of such posturing: principally American firms that lose market share in the targeted countries and innocent civilians (especially the poor) in those countries who often find themselves facing even leaner times than normal.

There are, of course, occasions when commerce may have to be restricted for legitimate national security reasons. Even Adam Smith recognized a national security exception to the general principle of free trade. The possibility that an American corporation may have helped upgrade the guidance systems of ballistic missiles for the People's Republic of China would certainly fall into that category.

But the national security exception has to be narrowly drawn lest it become a pretext to impose restrictions for far more mundane motives. Two key conditions ought to be present. First, the transaction in question must provide a direct and substantial boost to the military capabilities of a nation that could pose a credible security threat to the United States. Second, the American firm involved in the transaction must have a cutting-edge product or service that could not readily be supplied by firms in other countries. Admittedly, such standards are not self-implementing, and interpretation is both difficult and subjective in cases of dual-use technologies. Insistence on some reasonably specific security-based standards, however, would at least brake the enthusiasm for making trade relations subservient to an endless array of foreign policy pet causes.

It is painful enough for American businesses to accept the need to forgo commercial opportunities because of bona fide national security requirements. It is far worse to endure such interference when national security is not at stake. Unfortunately, that has been the frustrating experience in a growing number of cases.

There is little prospect that the hoary embargo against Cuba—or even the especially onerous provisions of the more recent Helms-Burton amendment—will be lifted anytime soon. Yet even the Pentagon concedes that the decrepit Castro regime no longer poses a security threat to the United States. Sanctions were placed on Serbia earlier this decade, not because that country is a menace to America's security, but because Washington objected to Belgrade's actions with regard to the civil war in Bosnia. More recently, restrictions were reimposed after a brief hiatus because Serbia has had the temerity to suppress a secessionist movement in one of its own provinces.[6] Burma is a target of sanctions because the government in Rangoon is undemocratic and treats political opponents harshly—a standard that, if applied consistently by Washington, would sever America's commerce with a majority of countries.[7] China is likewise the target of religious conservatives and the human rights lobby because of Beijing's repressive domestic policies. If the sponsors of congressional legislation have their way, any number of countries could be blacklisted for failing to practice sufficient religious tolerance—as determined by a new Office of Religious Persecution Monitoring in the U.S. State Department.[8]

Business leaders and others might justifiably wonder what issues of that nature have to do with the security of the American republic.

7

Yet that is the official rationale for all such existing or proposed restraints on trade and investment.

Not only are economic sanctions and other restrictions imposed for reasons that have nothing to do with legitimate national security concerns, they are often imposed even when there is virtually no prospect that they will achieve their stated objective. Few developments can be more maddening to American businesses than to be blocked from lucrative markets while firms based in other countries take advantage of Washington's myopia and rigidity. That was the case for two decades following the end of the Vietnam War as the United States vainly sought to isolate the Hanoi regime.[9] It remains the case today with regard to such countries as Cuba and Iran.[10]

Foreign policy officials and members of Congress have been slow to learn from such experiences and to appreciate the futility of emotionally driven crusades. That was illustrated with depressing clarity by Washington's initial response to the nuclear tests conducted by India and Pakistan in 1998. Instead of recognizing that the simplistic "just say no" nonproliferation policy the United States has pursued since the 1960s is no longer sustainable (a point understood by some scholars years ago),[11] the Clinton administration reacted with the foreign policy equivalent of a temper tantrum.

Admittedly, the administration did not have a great deal of latitude in crafting a response. The misguided 1994 Nuclear Proliferation Prevention Act required the imposition of sanctions against any nation that pursues a nuclear weapons program—much less tests such weapons. Some of the sanctions (the mandates to oppose new World Bank loans and terminate bilateral aid flows) might inadvertently benefit India and Pakistan by weaning those countries from the narcotic of foreign aid. Other sanctions, though, especially the restrictions on private bank loans and technology exports, had the potential to inflict economic pain—at least in the short term. They were also likely to embitter relations between America and both countries and cost American firms market share (only Japan and Canada among the G-8 countries agreed to go along with Washington's proposed sanctions strategy) without having any realistic chance of getting New Delhi and Islamabad to abandon their drive to acquire modest nuclear deterrents.

Despite the initial bipartisan enthusiasm for penalties against India and Pakistan, the episode shows signs of becoming a catalyst for a more realistic attitude about sanctions. Almost immediately, the administration began pressing Congress for more discretion in imposing sanctions, not only in response to the South Asia problem, but in other cases as well. The powerful agricultural lobby promptly and successfully sought a congressional exemption for food exports to India and Pakistan, and the Senate voted to give the president greater overall latitude. Even Sen. John Glenn (D-Ohio), principal author of the Nuclear Proliferation Prevention Act, conceded that the statute might be too inflexible, although he continued to oppose a broad waiver power for the executive. Sen. Richard Lugar (R-Ind.) and other sponsors attracted a surprisingly high level of support for general reform legislation on the sanctions question.

Such developments have sparked a wide-ranging debate on the efficacy of sanctions, with proponents (both in Congress and in the foreign policy community) clearly on the defensive.[12] It is too soon to tell whether the enthusiasm for sanctions has reached high tide and will now ebb, but these are the first encouraging signs of wisdom on the issue in many years.

Reinforcing the new domestic debate on sanctions is mounting international hostility to America's fondness for the tactic.

The refusal of other major economic powers to go along with some of Washington's more ill-advised campaigns of economic coercion is increasingly frequent and emphatic. Both the Executive branch and Congress have often responded petulantly. The most damaging reaction has been the attempt to give U.S. sanctions laws extraterritorial jurisdiction—i.e., to penalize foreign firms that defy or otherwise undermine sanctions that Washington has imposed on a target country. That was the case with both the Helms-Burton legislation and the sanctions measure against Iran. Washington's attempt to use the foreign policy equivalent of a secondary boycott has infuriated the governments of various European Union members as well as other countries and has led to threats of retaliation. Although cooler heads seem to be prevailing as the Clinton administration beats a tactical retreat, congressional militants are reluctant to abandon the strategy.[13]

Unless fundamental changes in U.S. foreign policy take place, the economic collateral damage—already considerable—is certain to grow. American businesses will run afoul of an ever-expanding array of restrictions on overseas trade and investment imposed in the name of national security but in reality serving the parochial agendas of various domestic political constituencies. In a broader sense, the American people will continue to be overtaxed and over-regulated so that Washington can pursue the unrealistic goal of a permanent global pax Americana.

There is a better way. The United States is easily the single most powerful country, both militarily and economically, in the international system. But even that vast power does not translate into an ability to dictate outcomes everywhere and under every circumstance. The United States cannot thwart all aggressors, secure human rights for all people suffering oppression, or export democracy at the point of a bayonet to recalcitrant societies. Indeed, America's most potent source of influence is the power of example based on a commitment to the values of individual rights and limited government. Playing the role of global hegemon, much less global bully, undermines those values and the influence that flows from them.

Washington needs to prune its grandiose ambitions and concentrate on the protection of vital American interests—a difficult enough task in a dangerous world. Above all, the notion that the economy should be the handmaiden of the national security state must be repudiated. As long as U.S. political leaders act as though overseas economic ties can be manipulated or casually sacrificed as pawns to advance foreign policy goals (and all too often, whims), the collateral damage of pax Americana will be far too high.

## Notes

1. Economic costs are, of course, just one part of the tally. The more than 100,000 American lives lost in the Korean and Vietnam wars, the corrosive effects of Washington's garrison state policy on civil liberties, and the rise of the imperial presidency are other important aspects of the price of global interventionism. For a discussion, see Ted Galen Carpenter, "Global Interventionism and Erosion of Domestic Liberty," *Freeman*, November 1997, pp. 660–65.

2. Robert Higgs, "The Cold War Economy: Opportunity Costs, Ideology, and the Politics of Crisis," *Explorations in Economic History* 31 (1994): 283–312.

3. Robert Higgs, *Crisis and Leviathan: Critical Episodes in the Growth of American Government* (New York: Oxford University Press, 1987).

4. Richard Lawrence, "Sanctions Fever," *Journal of Commerce*, June 3, 1998, p. 7A.

5. Nancy Dunne, "U.S. Congress Considering Wide Range of Sanctions," *Financial Times*, June 5, 1998, p. 3.

6. Toni Marshall, "U.S. Sanctions Serbia for Attacks," *Washington Times*, June 9, 1998, p. A15.

7. Leon T. Hadar, "U.S. Sanctions against Burma: A Failure on All Fronts," Cato Institute Trade Policy Analysis no. 1, March 26, 1998; Stuart Anderson, "Stop the Sanctions Game," *Journal of Commerce*, July 11, 1996.

8. "Religious Persecution Bill Passes House by Strong Margin," *CQ Weekly*, May 16, 1998, pp. 1324–25.

9. For an analysis of how Japanese corporations attained entrenched positions in Vietnam while the United States continued its diplomatic and economic cold war against that country, see Alan Tonelson, "Mitsubishi's Plan for Vietnam," *Washington Post*, July 11, 1993, p. C1.

10. Suzanne Possehl, "Embargo Costs U.S. Dearly as Cuba Tries Private Enterprise," *Journal of Commerce*, June 8, 1998, p. 1A.

11. See, for example, Ted Galen Carpenter, "A New Proliferation Policy," *National Interest* (Summer 1992): 63–72.

12. Recent examples of attacks on sanctions as a foreign policy tool include Richard N. Haass, "Sanctions Almost Never Work," *Wall Street Journal*, June 19, 1998, p. A14; "Sanity for Sanctions," editorial, *Journal of Commerce*, July 20, 1998, p. 6A; Nancy Dunne, "Sanctions Overload," *Financial Times*, July 21, 1998; and Robert A. Pape, "Why Sanctions *Still* Do Not Work," *International Security* 23, no.1 (Summer 1998): 66–77.

13. James Bennet, "To Clear Air with Europe, U.S. Waives Some Sanctions," *New York Times*, May 19, 1998; Holger Jensen, "Clinton Sanctions Deal," *Journal of Commerce*, May 26, 1998, p. 8A; and Nancy Dunne, "Helms-Burton Deal May Come Unstuck," *Financial Times*, June 2, 1998, p. 8.

# 2. An Overview of the Economic Costs of Unilateral Trade Sanctions

*William H. Lash III*

Observe an economic tragedy in the making. You have spent billions of dollars on establishing a first-rate corporation, employing thousands of workers worldwide. Your product is an industry leader and your technology is state of the art. In key emerging markets you have a market share of approximately 85 percent. Then, voilà, overnight you find that your government has placed two-thirds of the world's markets under sanctions, restricting your ability to sell. This story is not by horror *meister* Stephen King. The author of these repeated economic horrors is the U.S. government.

The estimated economic losses from unilateral trade sanctions are $15 billion to $20 billion in forgone exports annually. Though those figures are staggering, I believe that the true costs of unilateral sanctions are far greater. Economic losses fall in several camps: lost sales, lost market shares, lost technology, lost foreign investment, and higher costs to American consumers and taxpayers.

The types of sanctions are limited by only the imagination and the conscience of our political leaders. Current federal sanctions block U.S. firms from participating in nuclear power projects, defense trade, and satellite launch programs. They prohibit financial transactions and loans, restrict air travel and exports, impose embargoes, block foreign firms from federal procurement, deny General System of Preferences tariff treatment, and deny visas to corporate officers and their families.

Over 75 individual states, literally ranging from Angola to Zaire, are currently subject to or potentially targeted by U.S. unilateral economic foreign policy sanctions. Countries face sanctions for a

William H. Lash III is a professor of law and director of the International Business Law Program at George Mason University.

host of reasons ranging from having a communist government, environmental standards, expropriating or dealing in expropriated U.S. property, human rights standards, military actions or proliferation of weapons of mass destruction, drug trafficking, labor standards, and, my personal favorite, restrictive trade practices. After all, in the world of trade policy, two wrongs must make a right. Is there a better way to teach a trading partner the folly of restricted markets than by continually closing our own markets, harming consumers in both states?

Historically, many analysts point to the failed grain boycott of the Soviet Union in 1980 as the classic case of economic sanctions gone awry. The grain embargo imposed by the Carter administration did manage to raise the costs of grain to the Soviets by an estimated $225 million. But the Soviets were able to obtain grain from new sources and their military aggression in Afghanistan was not deterred. The economic cost to the United States was a loss of $2.3 billion in sales to the Soviet Union. The U.S. grain producers also lost their dominant vital market share in the U.S.S.R., a market position they were never able to recapture. The losses in this sector are perpetuated because the Russians fear becoming dependent upon U.S. producers subject to the political whims of the U.S. government.

Similarly, an effort to punish Soviet behavior in Poland led to an embargo against supplying goods and services to build the Soviet pipeline. The pipeline was constructed with Japanese suppliers while U.S. manufacturers like Caterpillar were cut out of the sale. Perhaps even more importantly, Caterpillar, which had enjoyed an 85 percent market share in the Soviet Union, lost that market share. Like the grain producers earlier, Caterpillar was viewed as being subject to a government in love with economic sanctions. In a global economy, people are less willing to gamble with the unpredictability of U.S. foreign policy and its economic ramifications.

A U.S. manufacturer of oil drilling equipment is a recent victim of the "sanctions fear factor." An opportunity to sell equipment and services to build an offshore oil rig in the North Sea was lost, not because of the fear of sanctions against Great Britain but because of the fear of U.S. sanctions precluding possible future transportation of the equipment to other, more politically sensitive countries.

The loss of sales where sanctions have not been threatened or imposed demonstrates the depth of the problem of unilateral economic sanctions. A fear of sanctions has led to many states viewing U.S. manufacturers as unreliable sources of supply and the United States as a nation that ignores the rights of private parties to freely contract. With other producers from Europe or the Pacific rim available, such losses will only mount. In industries such as telecommunications, U.S. producers account for only 16 percent of the world export market. In agricultural equipment, U.S. firms hold a 20 percent market share globally. Unilateral economic sanctions effectively cede many markets to our competitors.

Fear of U.S. unilateral sanctions also drives American firms from lucrative joint venture or supply opportunities. The amount of U.S. content in Airbus aircraft has dropped from 50 percent 25 years ago to less than 20 percent in 1992. Part of the reason for the decline was to escape onerous U.S. export controls. American firms recently lost an opportunity for participation in an international oil project in Azerbaijan because the U.S. government currently restricts international financing to Azerbaijan. The members of the joint venture excluded the U.S. firm because of fear that U.S. unilateral sanctions against the country might be expanded in the future, forcing the U.S. firm to withdraw abruptly.

These losses are only the tip of the economic iceberg. While the losses of initial sales are quite large, the follow-up sales of goods, equipment, and services are sales losses that will continue for decades. In large equipment and technology sales, these lost opportunities for future supply are staggering.

A 1994 Council for Competitiveness study concluded that $6 billion in exports, representing 120,000 export-related jobs, were lost from just eight unilateral sanctions. Research by the Institute for International Economics in 1995 determined that an estimated 200,000 to 250,000 export-related jobs were lost from unilateral sanctions against 26 countries. The studies do not account for the additional losses of follow-up sales.

These losses are particularly important for our economy. Trade-related jobs pay an estimated 17 percent more than other similar employment. Furthermore, trade is an increasingly large part of our economy. In the United States, 30 percent of Gross Domestic Product is internationally trade related. Twenty-five years ago only 13 percent of Gross Domestic Product was related to international trade.

If left unmolested, exports are projected to grow at a rate of 9.5 percent annually through the year 2000. Thus, unilateral economic sanctions threaten a larger part of our economy than ever before.

Our export markets are also undergoing new developments, making them more sensitive to unilateral sanctions. States designated as Big Emerging Markets by the U.S. Department of Commerce are expected to receive more exports than the European Union and Japan combined by the year 2000. Many of them, notably China, Mexico, Turkey, Indonesia, and India, are estimated by the U.S. Trade Representative to reach the same income level as Spain by 2010. Those potential markets are continually faced with running afoul of our multiplying sanctions mania.

Economic sanctions may lead to retaliation against U.S. firms. That retaliation may come in direct or more indirect forms. Can anyone deny that the Chinese purchases of Airbus aircraft were not strategically timed to send a message to Washington via Washington State?

The market for nuclear energy in China is estimated at $50 billion. The U.S. nuclear power industry views access to that market as crucial to its survival. Continued denial of market access will lead to tens of thousands of job losses in 28 states. Additionally, it is feared that a decline in the U.S. nuclear power industry will lead to a weakening of our base of trained employees, vital to the support of the Navy and 100 nuclear power plants.

The cumulative impact of trade sanctions should also include the cost of business never considered as well as the loss of potential foreign investment. Foreign-based multinationals, fearful of being subjected to U.S. export controls and sanctions policy, may consider establishing facilities in other, less sanctions-happy, locales. Those foreign subsidiaries account for 5 percent of all domestic employment. Additionally, the firms account for an estimated 22 percent of all U.S. exports. The current sanctions-prone environment may chill future foreign direct investment and cost the U.S. new jobs, technology, and access to foreign markets.

Another cost of sanctions includes higher prices and reduction of choices in areas such as government procurement. By closing our procurement markets we violate the World Trade Organization Agreement on Government Procurement, an agreement the U.S. so desperately sought during the Uruguay Round. Other economic sanctions restricting oil imports lead to higher costs for American firms and consumers.

According to an old fable, an eagle once was stricken by a dart. When it saw the fashion of the shaft and the use of its own feathers, the eagle noted, "It is by our own hands, and not by others, that we are now fallen." Let us hope that the American eagle will once again be free to fly in global markets with no fear of self-inflicted wounds.

# 3. Defending Liberty in a Global Economy

*Richard B. Cheney*

I want to thank Cato for hosting this conference today. I think it is extremely timely and exactly the kind of thing that your institute is very good at. I appreciate being asked to participate.

I want to speak to you today from two perspectives. First, from the standpoint of somebody who has been heavily involved in government, especially in broad issues concerning U.S. strategic and national interests around the globe. But I would also like to talk briefly from the point of view of someone who is currently serving as the CEO of a major corporation. First, let me take just about two minutes and give you a quick commercial on Halliburton so you will understand the kind of company we are and why we are interested in these issues.

Halliburton was founded some 70 years ago in Duncan, Oklahoma, by one man and a truck, cementing oil wells and casings inside oil wells. Over the years we developed the capacity to do everything downhole that is necessary to produce oil and gas: we drill wells, we do completions on wells, we cement, we stimulate, and we undertake a host of other activities involved in the production of oil and gas. We also own Brown & Root Engineering, a company that began about 70 years ago with two brothers with a road grader in Austin, Texas. Brown & Root is in the business of building offshore platforms, undersea pipelines, refineries, and other downstream facilities. Brown & Root is also heavily involved in the operations and maintenance business. They currently have the logistics contract for the U.S. Army in Bosnia, under which they build and operate all the camps for the U.S. Army deployed there.

Richard B. Cheney is the chief executive officer of Halliburton Company and the former U.S. secretary of defense.

19

As a measure of the company's diversity, I should also mention that we are building the new baseball stadium in Houston.

Halliburton recently merged with Dresser Industries to create a company of more than 100,000 employees, with revenues that put us among the top 100 companies in America. We are the largest private employer in Texas and operate in over 130 countries all over the globe. About 70 to 75 percent of our business is energy related, serving customers like Unocal, Exxon, Shell, Chevron, and many other major oil companies around the world. As a result, we oftentimes find ourselves operating in some very difficult places. The good Lord did not see fit to put oil and gas only where there are democratically elected regimes friendly to the United States. Occasionally we have to operate in places where, all things considered, one would not normally choose to go. But, we go where the business is. So, what happens with respect to U.S. commercial policy, how we conduct ourselves as a nation, the kinds of rules and regulations that American firms are expected to abide by and operate under, and how all of that affects our ability to compete overseas is of considerable interest to those of us at Halliburton. Obviously, such matters are not only important to our employees, but to our shareholders and our customers as well.

One of the things that I think is important for us to focus on for just a minute concerns the phenomenal changes that have occurred in the world in the last few years. When I was secretary of Defense, I spent part of my time targeting certain pieces of real estate inside what was then the Soviet Union. In early June of 1998, I was salmon fishing on the Kola Peninsula up near Murmansk and Archangel where the Soviet northern fleet has been based for years. In an astonishingly short period of time, the world has been so transformed that now a former U.S. secretary of Defense is perfectly free to hop on an airplane, fly over to the former Soviet Union, and spend a week salmon fishing. It is amazing when you think about that transition.

Another dramatic sign of the times: our engineering company, Brown & Root, has a contract with the U.S. Department of Defense to destroy SS18 missile silos in Kazakhstan. There was a time, not long ago, when we were afraid that the only way those missiles would be destroyed was with other missiles. Now we are cutting them up with acetylene torches! That sort of activity was incomprehensible just a few short years ago when I was still with the government.

There have obviously been phenomenal changes, not only in the political and military arena, but in the economic as well. I think much of the reason for such a remarkable transformation all over the globe is economic competition and the power of the ideas and the concepts that are embodied in the U.S. economy. The inability of the old centrally planned states such as the Soviet Union to compete economically, to provide the necessary resources for national security, and to meet the basic demands of its citizens ultimately drove them to the realization that they must fundamentally change their systems if they were going to survive.

I believe that economic forces have driven much of the change in the last 20 years, and I would be prepared to argue that, in many cases, economic progress has been a prerequisite to political change. The power of ideas, concepts of freedom and liberty and of how best to organize economic activity, have been an essential, positive ingredient in the developments in the last part of the 20th century. At the heart of that process has been the U.S. business community. Our capital, our technology, our entrepreneurship have been a vital part of those forces that have, in fact, transformed the world. Our economic capabilities need to be viewed, I believe, as a strategic asset in a world that is increasingly focused on economic growth and the development of market economies.

I think it is a false dichotomy to be told that we have to choose between "commercial" interests and other interests that the United States might have in a particular country or region around the world. Oftentimes the absolute best way to advance human rights and the cause of freedom or the development of democratic institutions is through the active involvement of American businesses. Investment and trade often can do more to open up a society and to create opportunity for a society's citizens than reams of diplomatic cables from our State Department.

I think it is important for us to look on U.S. businesses as a valuable national asset, not just as an activity we tolerate or a practice that we do not want to get too close to because it involves money. Far better for us to understand that the drive of American firms to be involved in and shape and direct the global economy is a strategic asset that serves the national interest of the United States.

One of the problems we face, I think, is that we have far too many policymakers who lack any real understanding of what the modern world economy is all about or how it actually functions. I am concerned that we have a lot of policymakers who may be wise in the ways of Washington but are, frankly, naive about the way the world economy works. I think they tend still to view international commerce as a process by which nations trade a few agricultural commodities and some manufactured goods and that is it. They believe that commerce is easily controlled and regulated by national governments, and that, if necessary, the United States can isolate itself from the rest of the world's economy and remain prosperous. That is what I call the "Pat Buchanan view" of international economics. Please understand: I like Pat Buchanan. Pat is a friend of mine. I thought Pat was a great speechwriter when he worked for Richard Nixon, and he is a fine TV commentator, but he is dangerous if he ever gets control of U.S. economic policy.

National boundaries simply do not mean what they used to mean economically. The vast flows of capital and technology, the Internet, the tremendous growth in services moving back and forth across international borders and between centers of economic opportunity and activity around the globe have dramatically transformed what we think of as the world's economy. We need enlightened political leadership that understands and comprehends the complexities of the world economy. All too often these days that leadership appears to be lacking.

I want to spend a few minutes this afternoon on my favorite hobbyhorse, the question of unilateral economic sanctions. Let me emphasize at the outset that I am not automatically, absolutely opposed to all sanctions. I think there are occasions when an appropriate policy response by the United States is to impose sanctions on some foreign government. But those occasions are relatively few. I think in most cases they are appropriate only where we can think in terms of multilateral sanctions, when there is something of an international consensus willing to follow U.S. leadership. Under those circumstances it may make sense to pursue a sanctions policy. I would cite, for example, what the international community has done with respect to Iraq in the period since the Gulf War as an appropriate use of multilateral economic sanctions.

But my concern today is primarily with *unilateral* economic sanctions imposed by the United States. I would begin by arguing that they almost never work. It is hard to find specific examples where they actually achieve a policy objective. Unfortunately, as has been pointed out repeatedly in recent public debate, our government has become "sanctions happy." I do not mean to be partisan here. I think there is plenty of blame to go around for both parties with respect to the question of the use of unilateral sanctions. But let me cite a couple of facts from a recent issue of *U.S. News & World Report*. In the last 80 years, the United States has imposed economic sanctions some 120 times. More than half of those 120 instances have occurred in the last five years, since the Clinton administration came to power. I do not know that there is any connection, but one cannot deny that, during that period, we have been far quicker to move in the direction of sanctions than ever before.

Currently, again according to *U.S. News*, we have got some 70 countries around the world affected by sanctions of one kind or another imposed by the United States. Those 70 countries are home to almost two-thirds of the world's population. Now, again, I might be willing to listen to arguments for the imposition of all those unilateral economic sanctions if somebody can produce significant evidence that they work. At a minimum, I would think such evidence ought to illustrate that we achieved the desired change that was used as the rationale when we adopted the sanctions in the first place. Typically, some government is pursuing a policy we do not like or we disagree with and we impose sanctions with the expectation that they will then understand we do not like that particular policy and they will change it. As a practical matter, it is almost impossible to find examples where in fact that has happened.

When we pursue those courses of action, the United States ends up in a position of adopting and advocating a policy that is almost guaranteed to be ineffective. It makes one wonder why the United States, on purpose, would want to consistently pursue policies that do not work. But that is what we do every time we fall back on the use of unilateral economic sanctions. They do not produce the desired result, in part because most of the time such policies are motivated primarily by domestic political considerations, by a desire to respond to pressure from some group or other here at home. They are rarely adopted with respect to whether or not they make sense in terms of overall U.S. foreign policy goals and objectives.

When I went to work for President Ford back in the summer of 1974, our first foreign policy crisis had to do with a dust-up between the Greeks and the Turks, who had gone to war over the fate of Cyprus. The response of the Congress at that point was to impose an arms embargo on Turkey. Now that was particularly interesting because Turkey was a NATO ally. We had solemn treaty obligations with the Turks. To be sure, we had almost exactly the same kind of relationship with the Greeks. They were also NATO allies. But we placed sanctions on Turkey and not on Greece. Why? It was not because it made sense from the standpoint of what was happening on Cyprus, or made sense from the standpoint of overall U.S. foreign policy. We sanctioned Turkey because the Greek-American lobby was significantly bigger and more effective than the Turkish-American lobby here at home. That is the sum total of why we did it. Ultimately, we were able to get it reversed. But it took numerous votes in Congress before we were able to turn it around.

That was an example from 24 years ago, but it continues to happen. Right now there are sanctions on Azerbaijan. We are not allowed to spend any U.S. government dollars in that country. That is not a response to what we perceive to be sound foreign policy in that part of the world. It is more specifically a reflection of a desire by Congress to respond to the concerns voiced by the Armenian-American community, which is bigger than the Azerbaijani-American community. As a result we currently have a prohibition against U.S. government money being spent in Azerbaijan.

The problem in part stems from the view by my former colleagues on Capitol Hill that sanctions are the low-cost option. They are the cheap, easy thing to do. It is not necessary to appropriate any taxpayer's money. It is not necessary to send any young Americans into combat. We are able to take a firm, aggressive action and do something about the outrageous behavior of the offending government and, many members believe, it does not cost a thing. But that is a shaky premise, at best. Even though that is the view one will hear bandied about in the cloakroom, it is a false notion that has serious consequences, in part because our sanctions policy oftentimes generates unanticipated consequences. It puts us in a position where a part of our government is pursuing objectives that are at odds with other objectives that the United States has with respect to a particular region.

An example that comes immediately to mind has to do with efforts to develop the resources of the former Soviet Union in the Caspian

Sea area. That is a region rich in oil and gas. Unfortunately, Iran is sitting right in the middle of the area and the United States has declared unilateral economic sanctions against that country. As a result, American firms are prohibited from dealing with Iran and find themselves cut out of the action, both in opportunities that develop with respect to Iran itself, and also with respect to our ability to gain access to Caspian resources. Iran is not punished by this decision. Numerous oil and gas development companies from other countries are now aggressively pursuing opportunities to develop those resources. That development will proceed, but it will happen without American participation. The most striking result of the government's use of unilateral sanctions in the region is that only American companies are prohibited from operating there. That is not a "cost-free" option.

Another good example of how our sanctions policy oftentimes gets in the way of our other interests occurred in the fall of 1997 when Saddam Hussein was resisting U.N. weapons inspections. I happened to be in the Gulf region during that time. Administration officials in the area were trying to get Arab members of the coalition that executed operation Desert Shield/Desert Storm in 1991 to allow U.S. military forces to be based on their territory. They wanted that capability in the event it was necessary to take military action against Iraq to get them to honor the UN resolutions. Our friends in the region cited a number of reasons for not complying with our request. They were concerned with the fragile nature of the peace process between Israel and the Palestinians, which was stalled. But they also had fundamental concerns about our policy toward Iran. We had been trying to force the governments in the region to adhere to an anti-Iranian policy, and our views raised questions in their minds about the wisdom of U.S. leadership. They cited it as an example of something they thought was unwise and that they should not do.

So, what effect does this have on our standing in the region? I take note of the fact that all of the Arab countries we approached, with the single exception of Kuwait, rejected our request to base forces on their soil in the event military action was required against Iraq. As if that were not enough, most of them boycotted the economic conference that the United States supported in connection with the peace process that was hosted in Qatar during that time. Then, having rejected participation in that conference, they all went to Tehran and attended the Islamic summit hosted by the Iranians. The nation that is isolated by our sanctions policy in that part of the globe is not Iran. It is the United States. And the fact that we have tried to pressure governments in the region to adopt a sanctions policy that they clearly are not interested in pursuing has raised doubts in the minds of many of our friends about the overall wisdom and judgment of U.S. policy in the area.

We often find ourselves now in a position of advocating secondary boycotts. I can remember when the United States was the preeminent *opponent* of secondary boycotts. We opposed them, for example, when the Arabs tried to impose secondary boycotts on companies that did business in Israel. We thought that was a terrible idea. Now secondary boycotts are part and parcel of the Helms-Burton Act and also of the Iran/Libya Sanctions Act. Sanctions provisions in both of those laws are extraordinarily clumsy policy tools, as illustrated by the fact that the administration has recently been waiving the provisions of both acts as not being in the interests of the United States.

The parochialism of the Congress in looking at these kinds of issues and responding to domestic political pressures, as opposed to pursuing what I would consider to be sound foreign policy, is not new. When I was a member of Congress, my constituents in Wyoming wanted me to worry about Wyoming. That is not surprising since that is part of the way in which our system was designed. We cannot always expect good national policy to be articulated by every member of Congress. But the president is expected to be the counterweight to that and to be able to stand up and be counted when necessary. The chief executive is supposed to take the hard-nosed position, to exercise the veto, to do what President Ford did back in 1974 with the Greeks and Turks, and what others have done subsequent to that. I would hope this Administration will be more aggressive in that regard in the future than they have been in the recent past.

I do want to say a word about some positive developments that I think are underway with respect to these issues on Capitol Hill. I am a big supporter of the Lugar bill. I think Sen. Richard Lugar (R-Ind.) and Congressmen Philip Crane (R-Ill.) and Lee Hamilton (D-Ind.) put together a good piece of legislation in S. 1413. The Lugar bill would bring sanity to the process by forcing a review of sanctions legislation, setting up sunset provisions, and assessing the effectiveness and economic impact of sanctions.

However, it is important for us not to assume that now, because there is a growing chorus of concern being voiced, we have made the case. There is still significant interest on the Hill in the use of unilateral sanctions. The House in 1998 passed a whole new set of sanctions based around the concept of religious persecution. Some of my friends in the House who supported the Wolf-Specter bill, H.R. 2431, tell me they do not really want to see it passed. They know that the Senate will kill it. Then I go over and talk to my friends in the Senate, and they say, "Who me?" The fact is that supporters of the legislation are sincere, well-meaning people who are concerned about the religious persecution issue. I do not mean to take anything away from the motives of many of those who do support these kinds of bills. But the net effect of their approach will be to add a whole new category of unilateral sanctions that will be ineffective in achieving their ultimate goals.

I have not stressed the commercial arguments against sanctions. And I will not bore you with giving you a long list of how difficult it is for an international company like ours to function when our partners overseas are periodically reminded that we may not be able to carry through on a particular project because somebody here at home decides to sanction the particular country involved—thus causing us to be viewed as an unreliable partner. There is a whole long, separate speech I could give on the difficulties U.S. firms encounter as a result of the use of unilateral economic sanctions and on the subsequent commercial and economic consequences to the U.S. economy. What I have tried to do today is make the *policy* case against sanctions. They do not work. And as long as they do not work I think it is important for us to continue to remind people that we need to have some concern for the efficacy of policy before we advocate it as something the United States ought to pursue. I think it is important for us to recognize as a nation the enormous value of having American businesses engaged around the world. To recognize that engagement does more to encourage democracy and freedom, to open up societies, to create opportunities for millions of people who up until now have not been able to participate, than just about anything else we can do. We should look upon the capacities and capabilities and the desire of American businesses to be involved around the world as a valuable asset and not as a club that we can use to punish those who disagree with policies or goals or objectives of the United States.

# PART II

# EXPORT CONTROLS

# 4. Export Controls: A National Emergency?

*James B. Burnham*

In case it had escaped your notice, the United States is in a state of national emergency. We know this because Executive Order 12924 of August 14, 1994, proclaimed it. And every year since, in August, the President of the United States reaffirms the Executive Order, solemnly taking note of "the unusual and extraordinary threat to national security, foreign policy and [the] economy of the United States in light of the expiration of the Export Administration Act of 1979."[1]

Some will argue that the controversy about nuclear testing in India and Pakistan strengthens the argument for a "national emergency" —and a more stringent export control regime. But a closer look reveals three truths contrary to these ideas:

- Proliferation controls are inherently weak, particularly if contrasted with timely, credible strategic political commitments.
- The threat of unilateral sanctions has been an abject failure. Some would even argue that the conventional arms embargo imposed on Pakistan in 1990 accelerated the development of that country's nuclear program.[2]
- Any attempt to expand the scope and intensity of the current control regime in response to developments in South Asia will have a trivial impact on the spread of nuclear proliferation— but a nonnegligible cost for U.S. citizens. I use "cost" here as much in the sense of freedom from intrusive and arbitrary government actions as in an economic sense.

We are indeed facing a crisis of sorts. But it has more to do with rampant confusion in our legislative and executive branches

James B. Burnham is the Murrin Chair in Global Competitiveness at the Graduate School of Business at Duquesne University.

of government about the purpose, effectiveness, and costs of export controls than any "extraordinary threat" to our national security, foreign policy, and economy. This confusion is manifest in the multi-year deadlock over the reauthorization of the Export Administration Act (EAA). And, perhaps even more worrisome, in the middle of all this confusion the permanent bureaucracy is conscientiously erecting an administrative and legal infrastructure that Kafka would envy—and private citizens should fear.

This essay explores the rationale and the political basis for export controls and concludes with a list of six guiding principles. Adoption of the six principles would advance the cause of better government policy and individual freedom in important ways.

## The Rationale for Controls

We impose controls on exports when one or more of these four basic rationales apply:

- When the item in question is "in short supply."
- When considerations of "national security" are deemed to require it.
- When doing so will impede the proliferation of nuclear, chemical, or biological weaponry.
- When controls will satisfy an expanding list of populist sentiments that find expression in an emotional moral imperialism that has been given teeth by our military power and economic strength.

Some of these rationales have a legitimate basis in a coherent theory of liberty and government. Others do not. All the arguments can and have been used to advance extremely narrow economic, ideological, and sectarian interests. At the same time, bureaucrats' efforts to administer an increasingly complex system of controls on exports create an extraordinary mass of burdensome—and potentially draconian—administrative law.

"Short supply" has a long and checkered record as a rationale for restricting exports. Adam Smith cut his teeth on 18th-century England's long list of prohibitions on anything that might injure English wool cloth manufacturers.[3] The embargo on U.S. exports of scrap iron in 1940 and the freeze on Japanese financial assets in July 1941 probably influenced the date for the Japanese attack on Pearl

Harbor.[4] Richard Nixon used "short supply" to stop U.S. soybean exports to Japan in 1973 and thereby helped to make Brazil a competing world-class supplier in the 1980s.

More recently, the Department of Commerce, bowing to pressure exerted by a typical Washington "odd couple"—home builders and timber conservationists—has issued Congressionally mandated regulations tightening prohibitions on log exports from publicly owned lands. As a result, no one can purchase timber from public lands if the purchase would "substitute" for log exports from privately held land made at any time during the previous two years.[5]

## The Arbitrary Nature of Dual-Use Controls

Few, if any, object to the federal government's controlling exports under national security or proliferation rationales when the exporter's private interest (e.g., of fighter aircraft or weapons-grade plutonium) is at odds with foreign policy objectives such as U.S. neutrality in a regional conflict. More controversy rages over "dual-use" exports, most visibly in computer hardware and cryptographic software, but affecting a far greater number of industries than is commonly recognized.

The successor to the cold-war-era Coordinating Committee on Multilateral Export Controls, the Wassenaar Arrangement, defines "dual-use" goods, distinguishing between "basic," "sensitive," and "very sensitive" dual-use exports. But any such definitional effort and the application of each definition to specific cases generate a multitude of essentially arbitrary decisions concerning what will or will not be covered by a control regime. In the final analysis, many historical examples show that over time, all such controls will be overcome: in the short run, by smuggling of the controlled item, if the incentives are great enough, and, in the long run, by the inevitable diffusion of technology.

Meanwhile, the business community becomes enmeshed in an expanding web of law, regulation, and threat built up by our export control apparatus, without anyone's having made a credible case for its effectiveness.

## A Case Study

Consider the actual case of a medium-sized manufacturing company in the water treatment business. While a fair percentage of its sales are exports, this company has no defense- or nuclear-related business. Yet *every* export order must pass through a carefully documented process (subject to government audit) requiring a multitude of screening decisions entailing determinations concerning the intended recipient of the product, use of product, and countries transited by the shipment.

Export control laws also cover technical data. So, when the employees of the firm in the United States want to discuss manufacturing processes or other operations with someone from their overseas operations or a supplier, they must determine whether or not such discussions will involve a foreign national and "protected information"; if so, they must apply for permission to hold such a conversation, a process which normally involves a minimum of 90 days.

Naturally, the firm must obtain an export license if they want to hire a foreign national, even as a summer intern or graduate student, who might come into contact with "protected information." Since the informal definition of protected information is "information which would not normally be disclosed to a competitor," the cautious employer will always get the license or avoid coming into contact with such individuals and the value they might bring the firm.

Finally, the broad reach of the export laws empowers any Washington regulator simply to telephone the firm, even when it holds a valid export license, and demand that the firm stop an outgoing shipment, cancel a supplier's visit, or such. The basis for the request need not be disclosed, presumably because it might originate from a classified intelligence source. There is no appeal from such a request, even though highly classified intelligence has no guarantee of being highly accurate.

A small firm learning of this plethora of regulations might well choose to stay out of international activities altogether. The ignorant—or the "damn the Feds"—firm will never seek approval and thus run the risk of losing all export "privileges."

### The Nature of Export Control Costs

I leave quantification of the overall cost of this web of regulation to others,[6] but offer below a survey of ways in which an individual firm can be affected by export controls.

- Direct cost of compliance: Staff, legal and consultant time; recordkeeping costs.

- Indirect costs: Added time to respond to requests for quotations; the increased uncertainty as to whether or not a specific item requires a certain type of license.
- Deterrent costs: Potential business or job applicants never considered or pursued, given an estimate of the added direct cost, time, and uncertainties that would be involved.
- Competitive costs: Order inquiries that are never made, ideas from foreign suppliers or consultants that never get exposure; the ability of foreign competitors to operate in an environment with far fewer controls than the U.S. firm.

In short, it seems extraordinary that while the United States constantly seeks to expand economic freedom and dismantle other countries' barriers to trade, we are consciously erecting a formidable and costly set of restrictions on our own exports. Furthermore, thanks to the constraints on sharing information with foreign nationals, these barriers can reduce our ability to apply foreign technology to purely domestic manufacturing or technical challenges.

A better understanding of the full cost of controls might reduce the enthusiasm for controls in the halls of Congress and the bowels of the bureaucracy. In particular, it might cool the ardor of the emotional moral imperialists in the Congress and on our talk shows for unilateral economic sanctions to advance the Cause of the Month.

But, because new controls require no significant budget expenditure or tax increase, and typically affect only a small number of companies, imposing new controls has become a relatively painless way for Washington to respond to political pressure from well-organized interest groups. Only recently has the business community begun to follow the high-performance computer sector in recognizing the mounting cost of export controls, particularly sanction-driven controls. Our civil libertarian community should take a deeper interest in this issue, as well.

The substantive substitute for export controls and sanctions— strategic political commitments backed by the credible promise of military intervention—has its own set of costs. But the United States clearly is prepared to make those commitments only in a limited number of cases—for example, NATO expansion.

### Six Principles for Export Controls

Perhaps the time is right to bring reason to bear on the confusion in Congress and elsewhere on the issue of export controls. Here are six general principles for consideration:[7]

1. The export of goods, services, and data by private parties to other countries should be viewed as normal commercial activity, so long as it is privately financed. It should not be regarded as a special privilege granted by the federal government.
2. When new controls are proposed, the prospective costs and benefits should be publicly detailed. A serious effort at cost-benefit analysis can make an important contribution to policy choices.
3. A substantive annual report from the Executive branch to Congress on the costs of existing controls should be provided. The existing reports, such as are included in the Bureau of Export Administration's annual report and the President's semiannual reports to Congress on "the national emergency caused by the Lapse of Export Administration Act" are trivial.
4. Exports of weapons and munitions capable of directly inflicting harm to others should continue to be controlled. Manufacturers of fighter aircraft and artillery shells are rightly subject to a high level of supervision for obvious foreign policy reasons.
5. No other exports should normally be subject to restriction unless all other countries capable of supplying the item in question also agree to forbid exports to the potential buyer. To have any hope of being effective in the short run, all potential exporters must agree on one course of action—and enforce the agreement. An exception should be made for exports that benefit from direct government assistance, e.g., financed by export subsidy programs of the Department of Agriculture, foreign aid, or the Export-Import Bank. Such exports should be liable to unilateral manipulations by their financial agency.
6. Otherwise, unilateral export controls should be considered only when the United States is prepared to engage in direct military action to achieve its objectives. For example, our response to the Iraqi invasion of Kuwait in 1990 would be covered by this principle. By establishing a very high (and credible) political "threshold" for unilateral controls, we can be sure they will be taken seriously. The failure of controls (and the threat of sanctions) in the absence of such linkage is manifestly clear in the Indian/Pakistani resumption of nuclear testing in 1998.

Reshaping existing legislation to conform to these principles would build a more informed, transparent, and credible export control regime—and minimize the intrusion of government into private activity. The result would be a more effective and less costly process than now exists.

## Notes

1. *Weekly Compilation of Presidential Documents*, 1997, pp. 1242–43.
2. Milt Bearden, former CIA officer in Pakistan, as quoted in *The New York Times*, June 1, 1998, p. A6.
3. *The Wealth of Nations*, Book II, chapter 8.
4. Thomas A. Bailey, *A Diplomatic History of the American People* (10th ed.) (Englewood Cliffs, N.J.: Prentice-Hall, 1976), p. 734.
5. *Federal Register*, April 10, 1998, p. 17814.
6. See, for example, the excellent work by J. David Richardson, *Sizing Up U.S. Export Disincentives* (Institute of International Economics, 1993).
7. An earlier version of this list appeared in my monograph, *The Heavy Hand of Export Controls*, Center for the Study of American Business, Contemporary Issue Series 67, August 1994, pp. 19–21.

# 5. An Export Control Agenda for the 21st Century

*William A. Reinsch*

We are in the midst of a time of unprecedented political and economic transformation. The Clinton administration has taken an aggressive role adapting U.S. export control programs and priorities to address these new realities. This essay surveys where we are going and where we have been.

## The End of Cold War Containment

The export control policy of the United States since the end of the Second World War was based on "technology containment" of the U.S.S.R. and its allies. The multilateral controls implemented under the Coordinating Committee on Multilateral Export Controls auspices were a critical element of western deterrence. COCOM controls were imposed by a relatively cohesive western alliance against a clearly defined group of adversary countries. The system proved effective for a number of reasons:

- COCOM members had a virtual monopoly on a range of commercial dual-use technologies such as computers and telecommunications. When a monopoly chooses not to sell its products, then countries who want those products have to make major capital expenditures to develop their own or attempt to import them illegally. Hindsight reveals that the U.S.S.R.'s industrial system was not organized to commercialize dual-use technologies efficiently.
- COCOM members shared a common understanding regarding the focus of our controls and the political will among our partners to target them. Licensing decisions for a range of West–East

William A. Reinsch is undersecretary for Export Administration in the U.S. Commerce Department.

transactions were based on a consensus of the COCOM membership. In essence, COCOM countries permitted extraterritorial vetoes of their domestic export licensing decisions in the interest of promoting a collective security objective.

- COCOM's objectives were realistic. COCOM did not expect to prevent the U.S.S.R. from obtaining rudimentary nuclear weapons capability. COCOM's goal was to ensure that the West maintained a technological lead and overall qualitative superiority in military systems. Since the Warsaw Pact nations outnumbered those of NATO in overall manpower and equipment, COCOM's job was to ensure that the West maintained a technological edge that provided the basis for overall military parity.

But the dissolution of the Soviet Union changed the geopolitical underpinnings of the COCOM system and has made western overall export policy goals harder to achieve. The United States and its western partners no longer target the states which formed the Warsaw Pact and now seek to expand rather than restrict high technology trade with the East. The bipolar struggle is behind us, so the rationale for maintaining a broad program of technology denial is behind as well. Our interest now is to bring these countries, including Russia, into the international security, economic, and political system. Part of that process is to end their economic isolation and integrate them into western economic structures. That means trade—not just because it is good for us economically, but because it is good for better East–West relations.

### Licensing in the New Era

Pursuing trade does not mean ignoring national security. Export controls are one of the tools we use to manage technology transfers to protect national security and advance our foreign policy. U.S. regulations allow for extensive review and denial of license applications in cases where a strategically sensitive item would make a "direct and significant" contribution to military or weapons of mass destruction capabilities.

Under the Clinton administration, we have significantly improved the export control process to rationalize and to strengthen the role of all agencies in the review process. The engine of this revitalized process is Executive Order 12981, issued in December 1995. E.O. 12981 gives the Departments of Defense, Energy, and State and the

Arms Control and Disarmament Agency the right to review any license of interest to them. It establishes a clear system for escalation and resolution of disputes, and it provides for an appropriate review of technology transfer cases by the intelligence community. As a result, our license review is more thorough and more complete than at any time in the past.

### The Crisis of Instability

When the Soviet Union collapsed, economies and social infrastructure systems designed almost exclusively to support military procurement faced the massive task of conversion to civil applications. During the conversion, millions of people who supported the Soviet military machine faced severe economic privation and lacked a social "safety net" to ease the transition. Because their near-term choices were severely limited, many found the allure of selling sophisticated military hardware and know-how to foreign purchasers compelling. The more desperate their situation, the greater their willingness to sell to anyone willing to pay. Further, topnotch scientists and engineers found themselves without work in military enterprises and might have been willing to work for anyone prepared to offer employment. Russia's continuing difficulties have made this a long-term rather than a short-term problem.

Working with countries facing these problems to develop effective export controls and defense conversion promotes a wide range of U.S. security, trade, and political objectives. They include stemming the international proliferation of materials and technologies with application for weapons of mass destruction and limiting other destabilizing technology transfers to regions of concern.

The United States and other western nations must continue to support the development of democratic and market institutions without condescending paternalism. We face powerful nations undergoing difficult times. The West needs to support their march toward democracy and economic reform without appearing to be highhanded, as a patronizing attitude on our part strengthens the hand of those who argue that greatness lies in restoring the past rather than forging a new future.

### New National Security Challenges

The security challenges we face today are in many respects more complicated than those we faced during the cold war, and the solutions are less apparent.

First, the adherents to the major nonproliferation regimes (Missile Technology Control Regime, Australia Group, and, to a lesser extent, the Nuclear Suppliers Group) do not have a monopoly on many of the items they control. Therefore, countries seeking to develop weapons of mass destruction often can find alternative suppliers to fill their orders. Many of the countries can themselves manufacture items controlled by the regimes. It is fruitless to develop long lists of controlled items readily available from many suppliers in the world market. The longer the list of items, the more difficult it becomes to develop a meaningful consensus to implement effective multilateral export controls.

Second, we do not have a fully adversarial relationship with all the targets of our proliferation controls. On the contrary, we are seeking to engage those states in a dialogue to lead to closer integration with the international community and to develop a range of normal trade relations. Our goal is to restrict a very narrow range of transactions that could assist the countries' weapons development programs. To further complicate matters, our partners in the various nonproliferation regimes do not always share our views regarding which transactions should be restricted to which destinations, nor do we agree as to which countries or projects could pose strategic threats.

Unlike COCOM, there is no consensus today as to which countries should be the target of our controls. The preferred approach among our allies is to identify specific projects and seek to deny them technologies which could clearly contribute to weapons of mass destruction.

In that regard, we need to identify specific "chokepoint" items that can be effectively denied through multilateral cooperation and ensure that we have effective licensing and enforcement mechanisms to make the system work. Such lists must be developed strictly on nonproliferation policy grounds. As countries develop export control lists, they must resist the temptation to use the lists to seek competitive advantage in the international marketplace. This principle was more honored in the breach by COCOM, but a renewed emphasis on mutual security concerns could perhaps avoid the problem.

Note, interestingly, that the Nuclear Suppliers Group no longer controls computers because they are not considered to be chokepoint technologies for the development of nuclear weapons. Further, given the diffusion of computer technology around the world, it has become difficult to control such exports effectively, even on a multi-lateral basis. Indeed, machines that we classified and controlled as supercomputers just a few years ago are now on sale at retail stores for less than $1,000. Although the United States still maintains unilateral nuclear controls on computers, we must understand that the effectiveness of such a regime is limited.

Also complicating the issue is the blurring of the line between military and civilian goods and technologies. Part of this blurring is the increasing reliance of the military on commercial off-the-shelf technologies. There are real advantages to using commercial technologies, which may be better and are often cheaper than technology specifically made for the military. The other part is growing civilian demand for what were originally military technologies. Radiation-hardened chips for commercial communications satellites are a good example. Both trends complicate the task of fashioning rational export controls by creating broad-based civilian demand for products that also have critical military applications. Pressure to decontrol due to growing demand increases at the very time the military is increasing its reliance on the same products. Our national security interest lies more in making sure we maintain healthy high-tech companies that can supply our military's needs than it does in attempting to "control the uncontrollable."

## The Multilateral Solution

The solution to these problems is an old one—a multilateral approach.

In the final analysis, the extent to which multilateral control regimes can be effective is governed by each partner's willingness to consider proliferation as a major—if not principal—threat to both world security and its own national interests. Accordingly, we need to build regimes capable of denying proliferators the items they seek. Specifically, this includes doing the following:

- Identifying specific projects of concern.
- Drawing up a common list of items that will be subject to control.

43

- Implementing catchall provisions as a part of each country's legal and regulatory system, so that exports of any items destined to proliferation projects can be denied—regardless of whether they are specifically set forth on control lists.
- Sharing export licensing information in a timely manner so that "no undercut" agreements can be implemented—no member country should approve a sale of an item that a partner has denied.
- Imposing penalties sufficient to deter and punish violators.
- Committing adequate domestic resources for effective licensing reviews and enforcement.
- Administering active industry outreach programs so that companies understand their obligations.

**Conclusion**

The end of the cold war eliminated a major threat to U.S. and world security but has produced a host of new and multifaceted military, economic, and political challenges. The answer to each new problem that arises is not always clear—but the ultimate objectives certainly are:

- To maintain and promote American security and foreign policy interests in a world where very real threats are no longer posed by a monolithic bloc.
- To limit regulatory burdens on U.S. industry consistent with security and foreign policy objectives—regulations that cannot be justified based on material contributions to these national interests should be eliminated. New regulations and regimes that do not pass a strict effectiveness test should not be imposed in the first place.
- To enable defense-related industries to remain healthy in making the transition from a cold war environment to an era in which the volume of military procurement will be sharply reduced, yet still produce leading edge technologies.
- To support countries establishing democratic institutions based on acceptance of recognized standards of responsible international behavior—and to restrain countries who refuse to abide by internationally accepted norms.

We may be tempted to try to force the national security paradigm of the cold war upon today's world. However, I do not believe that any country still fits this paradigm—and cries for a return to past practices, no matter how strident, will not change this fact. The problems posed by the new international order are not amenable to simple or parochial answers. The best policy is one that moves in the direction of building alliances rather than enemies, and an export control agenda for the next century must reinforce it.

# 6. Export Controls, Trade Sanctions, and the Nuclear Industry

## R. Ian Butterfield

A senior staffer in the leadership of the House of Representatives recently joked—"This is not an isolationist Congress. We are fully internationally engaged. We will put sanctions on anyone!"[1] Apparently the House has thus achieved what the press repeatedly tells us the public wants—comity, civility, and bipartisanship, in that both parties seem to have gone sanctions crazy together.

The remark, of course, concerns trade sanctions. This nation is often reluctant to exercise the more traditional form of sanctions when we perceive our interests to be threatened—military sanctions. Instead, we typically turn to trade sanctions. In a sense, though, these are not sanctions at all, in the true sense of the term; implicit in the term "sanction" is the concept of force, of punishment. Merriam Webster's definition is "a coercive measure, usually taken by several nations together." But modern-day trade sanctions are fundamentally noncoercive. In a diversified global economy, where concepts of national security and self-interest are even more diversified, the United States can seldom win any significant international support for any of the trade sanctions it chooses to impose. Targeted nations denied access to U.S. goods are not, in fact, "sanctioned" at all, because they suffer no punishment. Goods and services they might ordinarily obtain from the United States are obtained from our Canadian, European, and Asian trade rivals. In short, if trade sanctions are not multilateral—and when are they?—they are, in reality, merely trade *gestures*. The targeted party suffers no pain. The truly sanctioned parties are the U.S. producer and the U.S. worker, who are denied the ability to market their goods and services in certain overseas markets.

R. Ian Butterfield is the director of government and international affairs at Westinghouse Electric Corporation.

### Sanctions an Expression of National Pique

This scenario is bleak, but the reality may be worse than its depiction. On occasion, we resort to so-called trade sanctions as a palliative when we are reluctant to take the more challenging and rigorous military option. But, unfortunately, the U.S. Congress now appears willing to legislate trade sanctions when only minor U.S. interests are under threat, or even when no U.S. interests are endangered whatsoever. Under those circumstances, sanctions have become not so much a foreign policy tool as an expression of national pique. We appear baffled by the complexity of a multipolar security and trading system and infuriated by the fact that the sovereign entities making up the global mosaic resolutely refuse to fall into line, follow our lead, and do what we tell them.

Indeed, one wonders if there were, indeed, somewhere out there, a mythical nation or nations willing to follow the U.S. lead on all occasions, how would it know what that lead was? As it crafted its policy towards Central America, would it listen to the Republican or Democratic party? In determining its relations with China, would it heed the U.S. Congress or the Clinton White House? Will it listen to the U.S. media? In short, we grow angry with, and levy sanctions on, countries who we believe have defied our will when, very often, we do not even have a unified national expression of that will.

Nor have we any consistent principles to determine when we will or will not levy trade sanctions. We have established or seriously threatened trade sanctions against various foreign countries for any of the following reasons:

- they do not share the U.S. understanding of the relationship between the individual and the state;
- their police forces do not conduct themselves as we would like;
- they discriminate against religious minorities;
- they do not accord trade unions the rights that they enjoy in the United States;
- they make overseas investments in places we do not like;
- they catch fish in a manner of which we disapprove;
- they trade with the wrong people or they trade with the right people but in the wrong things.

In drawing up this list, I am sure of only two things. First, if we set our minds to it now we could come up with a much longer and comprehensive list. Second, the list is going to get longer, particularly as the environmental movement presses for a global agenda.

## The Global Market Demand for Nuclear Power

The increased use of sanctions has had a significant impact on the U.S. nuclear industry and the global energy sector. Nuclear power plants are designed to add to a nation's baseload capacity to generate power. Currently, the world's developed economies in North America and Europe have very little demand for new baseload generation capacity. They have most of the power they need. Such demand as exists is for so-called "peaking capability," for generation systems that respond to temporary spikes in demand. Combustion turbines fueled by natural gas provide the most sensible, economic response to market demand for peak energy. There is, of course, a large market for nuclear goods and services in the developed world, and the market for nuclear power will grow again as existing baseload capability in developed economies ages and these economies seek to simultaneously replace aging capability and reduce greenhouse gas emissions.

But in many of the world's developing economies, the demand for new baseload capacity is high today. Some of the countries already possess domestic energy resources that render nuclear power uncompetitive, while others have a strong demand for nuclear power but lack the domestic resources to finance development. Foremost among the nations that demonstrate both a high demand for nuclear power and a manifest capability to finance the development of a nuclear infrastructure are China and India. Of course, the Westinghouse Company and, I am sure, the rest of the U.S. nuclear industry recognize that no nuclear business will be done in India until that country accedes to the Nuclear Nonproliferation Treaty or otherwise resolves its differences with the world community over its nuclear arsenal. Consequently, the analysis below is restricted to the Chinese market.

China has a huge demand for electricity. As controversy in the United States rages over the transfer of high technology to China, we easily forget that, overall, China is a low-tech, developing nation. Ten percent of the Chinese population, 120 million people, have no access to electricity whatsoever. My own conversations with groups such as the State Development and Planning Commission make it clear that bringing those people into the grid and generating power to supply that vastly expanded grid is one of the Chinese government's highest domestic priorities. If they fail to meet that objective they will be unable to slow the flood of people leaving the countryside for the industrial cities of the eastern seaboard, a critical problem. To bring electricity to that portion of the population that has none, the national and provincial authorities must, simultaneously, increase the amount of power available to those who already have access to the grid and respond to the steeply ramping demand from industry, particularly in the eastern industrialized provinces. What all this means is that China needs to grow its installed electrical generation base from 200 gigawatts today to 1,200 gigawatts by 2020, i.e., a 500 percent growth rate.

As China implements its massive program, its options are severely constricted by a variety of factors over which it has little or no control. First, it has little natural gas. Second, it has little oil. Third, while it has large reserves of coal, the coal is of very poor quality and is in the wrong part of the country, the west, far away from its manufacturing sectors. Currently, more than 50 percent of China's rail traffic is dedicated to the movement of coal. Naturally, the transportation costs greatly increase the overall cost of generating electricity through coal burning. Meanwhile, as anyone who has been to Beijing well knows, urban air pollution is rising exponentially. Chinese authorities are also beginning to compute associated health care costs into their calculations of the cost of coal-fired generation.

Bad news for China overall is good news for the nuclear sector. The factors outlined all make nuclear and hydroelectric power highly competitive in the Chinese marketplace. China now plans to expand its nuclear sector. Currently, nuclear power accounts for less than 1 percent of the country's power generation sector. By 2020, China wants to see nuclear power account for 5 percent of overall generating capacity. That might seem a humble goal, until one realizes it requires a 60-gigawatt program at an approximate cost of $100 billion to $120 billion. Approximately half that amount will go to whichever foreign exporter or exporters China chooses to work with in developing the nation's nuclear sector.

This should constitute an enormous opening for the U.S. nuclear industry. U.S. plants are, quite rightly, recognized as the safest, most reliable, and most efficient in the world. Certainly, China recognizes this and wants to buy U.S. plants. This is an industry that U.S. companies can dominate, generating 5,000 domestic engineering and manufacturing jobs with each plant sale.

## The Errors Behind U.S. Sanctions

What has been the U.S. government response to this enormous market opening? Until March 19, 1998, U.S. companies were not allowed to sell nuclear plants, fuel, or services in China. A *de facto* sanction exists because of Congress's failure to pass the U.S.-China Agreement for Peaceful Nuclear Cooperation, a bilateral treaty that is a prerequisite for any U.S. cooperation with or sales to any foreign country. President Reagan sent the treaty to Congress in 1985, but Congress refused to implement it until the President made certain certifications regarding Chinese conduct in the area of nuclear nonproliferation.

What was wrong with that? Certainly, no one wants to see nuclear weapons proliferate around the globe. The Congress had, in fact, made three serious mistakes. First, as usual, the U.S. stance was unilateral. Second, it made a mental connection between civilian nuclear plants and nuclear weapons that does not, in reality, exist. Third, it overlooked the fact that China is an internationally recognized legitimate nuclear weapons state.

To expand on the first point, unilateral sanctions make a mockery of Congress's position. No nuclear supplier nation in the world was willing to conform with the U.S. position. Consequently, while the U.S. government was denying U.S. vendors access to the Chinese marketplace, French, Canadian, and Russian vendors were all eagerly pushing their product in Beijing. To date, Framatome of France has built and signed contracts for reactors worth a total of $8 billion. Prime Minister Chrétien of Canada has visited Beijing and come away with a $2 billion order for AECL of Canada, and China has just signed a $4 billion contract with Minatom of Russia. Most, or even all, of this business could have gone to U.S. companies.

Second, in denying U.S. companies access to the China market, Congress overlooked the fact that the light-water reactors that all U.S. companies sell have virtually no proliferation implications. Proliferating nations that choose to build a uranium bomb do not need a reactor. Those who choose the plutonium route have always opted for a heavy-water plant, as did India, or a graphite-moderated plant, as did North Korea.

Third, and most annoying of all, China is an internationally recognized nuclear weapons state. Like the United States and Russia, it operates military reactors to supply material for its arsenal. Why, then, would it ever want to follow the devious, expensive, counterintuitive route of diverting material from light-water plants to its military complex? In this context, no one has ever alleged that China has diverted any material from the French light-water plants already in operation.

## Conclusion

The bulk of the world market for new nuclear plants in the next 10 to 15 years is in China. New plants will be built in Japan, but the bulk of that work will go to Japanese companies. So far as concerns U.S. companies, access to the Chinese market is the key to their survival as providers of new plants. Denied access to that market, with little chance of selling new plants for 10 to 15 years, any chief executive officer will wonder whether his company should stay in the new plant business or whether he should simply strip the deadwood off his company and become a simple fuel and services provider. Most of us would like to see the United States maintain some domestic new plant capability, particularly if we share the belief that nuclear power will have to play a notable role in combating greenhouse gases.

In asking for relief from export controls, the U.S. nuclear industry is not asking for a handout. No one is saying that the federal government needs to come to the aid of a distressed U.S. nuclear industry. The key to the future health and prosperity of the U.S. new nuclear plant industry is simply allowing it to compete on equal terms with its major international rivals in the main market for its products.

## Note
1. Conversation with the author.

# 7. Myths and Realities of the Debate over Encryption Policy

*Carl Ellison*

The mass-market deployment of strong encryption is essential to protect electronic networks against espionage and hackers. The U.S. government currently restricts the export of encryption stronger than 56 bits, except to certain industry sectors in certain countries. In many cases, the export of stronger encryption products is allowed only if the exporter guarantees government access to the keys that would enable law enforcement to decipher the encrypted message, abbreviated as government access to keys (GAK).

The debate about encryption export controls and the circumstances under which those controls might be lifted has been ongoing for 20 years now. We are tempted to believe that it is somehow new and current, because the arguments take new forms and the identities of those involved change. Proponents of continued export controls on encryption often ignore the history of both cryptography and cryptography policy. Recently, Principal Associate Deputy Attorney General Robert Litt revealed that he had never read the National Research Council's report on cryptography policy, "Cryptography's Role in Securing the Information Society," apparently because it had been written before he got involved in the issue.[1]

The debate also suffers from the attempts of proponents of regulation to cloud the policy debate in inflammatory or euphemistic rhetoric. Early proponents of guaranteed government access to keys called the process "key escrow," borrowing a term from the purchase of a family home, possibly to make it sound more palatable. Proponents of continued regulation assert that criminals will soon use encryption in massive numbers to impede law enforcement. But a study by Dorothy Denning and William E. Baugh Jr. (formerly of the FBI) found that today, "Most of the investigators we talked to did not

Carl Ellison is a cryptographer at Intel Corporation.

find that encryption was obstructing a large number of investigations. When encryption has been encountered, investigators have usually been able to get the keys from the subject, crack the codes, or use other evidence."[2] Also, proponents of GAK are fond of describing the use of encryption in crimes so disgusting (kiddy-porn-snuff films, for example) that the very image likely will upset a normal American listener so much that all rational thought about encryption issues ceases.

## The Myths and History of Cryptography

One FBI presentation on cryptography policy includes a figure showing the history of cryptography starting in about 1950, with government domination of the entire field until civilians entered the arena in the 1970s, developing DES and public key encryption. This is a convenient window for the history of cryptography, if one intends to show that encryption was always government property and one needs to reassert government control in some manner.

In fact, historians trace the history of cryptography to 1900 B.C. Over the centuries, civilians have consistently invented and used the strongest cryptographic systems.[3] Even in the 20th century, civilians had parity with government cryptographers. In 1917, a civilian named Vernam, working for AT&T, invented the first truly unbreakable cipher, the One Time Tape machine. This machine was put on the open market in 1920.[4]

Although civilians have always created the strongest systems, they have not always used the systems in large numbers. Historically, the most frequent user of cryptography, especially for communications, has been the government. But civilians have been the most frequent users of cryptography for storing documents.

The reason for the split has not been documented. It might be because, until recently, cryptography has been a laborious process, not likely to hold the interest of civilian users. Governments, on the other hand, were doing enough cryptanalysis to understand the need for encryption, and had the money to hire cipher clerks whose job was to perform the labor of enciphering and deciphering messages.

For secure storage of data, governments could call on armed guards, heavy safes, and so forth. A lone civilian, such as the potter who used encryption to preserve secrets of his glazes in 1500 B.C.[5]

had no such resources and would rely on cryptography to keep his secrets safe in storage.

### The History of the Encryption Policy Debate

Some people trace the cryptography policy debate back five years to the April 16, 1993, announcement of the Clipper Chip. More properly, the debate goes back at least to 1978, when Rear Admiral Bobby Inman, then director of the National Security Agency (NSA), proposed that cryptographic research be "born classified," as atomic energy research is. He wanted the NSA to control all cryptographic research in the United States. In making this request, he became the first director of the NSA to speak publicly about cryptography, apparently in reaction to the publication by Diffie and Hellman and then by Rivest, Shamir, and Adleman of papers describing the fundamentals of public key cryptography. Congress reviewed Inman's request and concluded that the NSA had no proprietary rights in this area; there was no reason to consider cryptographic research "born classified."

Inman then proposed that civilians voluntarily submit publications for prior review by the NSA. As recently as 1995, employees of the NSA spoke as if this policy were in effect and working. But the immediate result of the proposal at the time was to inspire the founding of two international journals of cryptography (*Cryptologia* and *The Journal of Cryptology*). Both accepted papers without prior review by NSA.

In the 1980s, the NSA started the Commercial Communications-Security (COMSEC) Endorsement Program, designed to provide classified, NSA-designed cryptographic devices for commercial products, devices that would use keys generated by the NSA. The program failed to gain widespread acceptance.

In 1991, the Administration proposed that Congress pass a resolution to the effect that when communications are enciphered, law enforcement should have a back door to the clear text of that communication. The proposal was defeated in Congress, but it raised warning flags in the minds of civilians. The primary result of the attempt was that Phil Zimmermann wrote and gave away copies of the first version of his program Pretty Good Privacy (PGP). PGP has since proliferated around the world.

In 1993, the Administration proposed the Clipper Chip—a device with a classified algorithm designed by the NSA. Clipper would use keys provided by the user, but would deliver those keys to any eavesdropper in possession of the master escrow key for the encrypting chip. Those master keys would be kept in government repositories, split into halves (each half useless by itself).

Clipper was a failure for the Administration, but inflamed the computer and communications community and the public. Sales of civilian cryptographic applications and devices started to ramp up rapidly. Every newspaper or magazine article addressing encryption issues promoted awareness of the threat to privacy from government eavesdroppers.

In 1994, Trusted Information Systems demonstrated a software-only version of Clipper. That program evolved into one useful for civilians in recovering their own keys. The Administration momentarily adopted this commercial offering as the new direction in cryptography policy. But the Trusted Information Systems model was not designed to provide access to a user's fundamental keys (private, key-exchange keys) or to provide easy, rapid, covert access to any keys. Instead, the Administration settled on a plan first proposed by cryptographer Silvio Micali. Under the Micali plan, a user would store his or her fundamental keys with a Trusted Third Party. The Trusted Third Party would issue identity certificates to the user and release the user's keys to the government. The industry has rejected this proposal, like all the others designed to give government access to keys.

In May of 1996, the National Research Council released "Cryptography's Role in Securing the Information Society," a report commissioned by Congress. The report's primary recommendations were these:

- No law should bar the manufacture, sale, or use of any form of encryption within the United States.
- National cryptography policy should be developed by the executive and legislative branches on the basis of open public discussion and governed by the rule of law.
- National cryptography policy affecting the development and use of commercial cryptography should be more closely aligned with market forces.

From Inman's first attempt to seize control of cryptography, through the Clipper incident, the result of the government's failure to follow the principles described above has consistently stimulated the public and the cryptographic community to resist. Cryptography journals, PGP, and the boom in cryptography sales thanks to Clipper have all hurt the stated interests of the Administration.

The policy debate over cryptography appears to be more a struggle for power than a rational pursuit of clear objectives. This might be a byproduct of a policy whose objectives remain classified. But in view of the National Research Council report's conclusion that the debate can be conducted in open, public discussion, there is no reason to assume any overpowering, classified reasons for the continuation of export controls and the pursuit of government access to keys.

### Realities of the Recovery of Keys to Stored Data

Even in the face of the fears and rhetoric surrounding this debate, some realities should be kept in mind. Civilians will need to recover their own keys for stored enciphered data. That data has value and without the key the data is lost. Therefore, the key that deciphers that data acquires the value of all the data it deciphers. This value can grow quite large. Therefore, an individual will need to make sure that decipherment keys for stored data are available into the indefinite future.

This is a problem in fault tolerance, complicated by the need for secrecy. A mechanism for achieving the long-term recovery of a user's personal secret key is available in the public domain.[6]

One of the reasons cited for taking recovery of keys out of the hands of individual users is the potential for a user to hold corporate data hostage by enciphering it. As Whitfield Diffie has pointed out, a corporation that allows any single individual to either keep all the data she or he generates or to have single-handed control over corporate data archives probably deserves to be victimized, as a punishment for improper management of corporate resources. A rogue employee could as easily delete corporate data as encipher it, if that employee wants to hurt the corporation. Anyone who wants to hold data hostage can steal it and keep it in a hidden location. A responsible company needs to institute policies to prevent single-person control over such valuable corporate resources as a master database or a programmer's work product. Those policies do not demand corporate access to individual employee cryptographic keys.

### Realities of Key Recovery for Communications

There is no reason for recovery of communication keys. A communication has no value per se, as Whit Diffie has pointed out. If the communication is broken by loss of a cryptographic key or for any other reason, the parties involved need only institute a new communication under a new key. They can do that faster than they can fetch a copy of the lost key from some key recovery center. The only entity that benefits from the potential recovery of communication keys is a government surveillance agent.

### Trusted Third Parties for a Public Key Infrastructure

In promoting the plan for public key infrastructures that would release master keys to government surveillance agents, the Administration's Interagency Working Group on Cryptography Policy noted in 1996 that "without a [public key infrastructure] of trusted certificate authorities, users cannot know with whom they are dealing on the network." But users do not need public key infrastructures or trusted certificate authorities (other than themselves) to identify those they already know on the network.[7] Even in dealing with strangers, users may need certain knowledge about the keyholders with whom they deal, but they cannot by definition know with whom they are dealing because that keyholder is not among the people that user knows. If a user orders a product from Company X, the user has no reason to care whether Company X is operated by Bob Smith or Jane Doe, so long as Company X sends the goods.

### Signals Intelligence

Proponents of GAK often cite the phenomenal importance of our cryptanalytic successes in World War II against the German and the Japanese machine ciphers, Enigma and Purple, respectively. This success was indeed important. The proponents of GAK forget one key component of those successes, however. All cryptanalytic successes depend on the enemy's having no hint that we are breaking their ciphers. Any such hint will cause them to either change their ciphers or encode information within the cipher so that if it is broken, it yields no information to us. Any public GAK attempt violates that lesson and therefore threatens signals intelligence by both the NSA and the FBI.

## Crypto and the Balance of Political Power: Attempt versus Success

Given the realities described and the weakness of the case for continued export controls and pressure to deploy government access to keys, what continues to drive the encryption policy debate?

The primary issue in the debate over encryption regulation is the balance between the right to attempt and a guarantee of success. Up to the present time, civilians have the ability and the right to attempt to keep secrets from others, including the government, by using strong cryptography. They do not, however, have a guarantee of success.

Meanwhile, the government has the right, with probable cause and a warrant, to attempt to penetrate the encrypted secrets of civilians. Government agents do not, however, have a guarantee of success. If either side were to be given a legal guarantee of success, then the other side would lose its right to attempt, since an attempt might succeed and therefore violate the other side's guarantee of success.

All GAK proposals to date have had as their goal the guarantee of success by government agents. What is driving the attempt to overthrow the balance? Perhaps a kind of machismo. The NSA enjoyed what it thought of as a monopoly in effective cryptography, from its founding in the 1950s to the present, but saw that monopoly threatened by civilian research papers in the 1970s. The FBI has enjoyed what it thinks of as unrestricted access to the cleartext of telephone conversations, through wiretaps, since those were made legal in 1968, and has since seen that source of information threatened by civilian cryptography. The FBI's demands in response to the threat seem inflated out of all proportion, as if the mere possibility that a surveillance target might successfully say "Nyah, nyah, I got a secret, and you can't see it" infuriates FBI policy makers beyond reason. Neither the FBI nor the NSA had any natural right to unchallenged superiority in code-cracking, but such superiority was implicit in the technology of the past decades, and any threat to this superiority was taken as if it were a threat to the survival of the

59

agencies themselves. The realities of the technology, however, demand that the agencies adapt to the new world rather than struggle to suppress it with new powers.

## Notes

1. Statement made at EPIC's "Cryptography and Privacy Conference," Washington, June 8, 1998.

2. William E. Baugh and Dorothy Denning, "Encryption and Evolving Technologies: Tools of Organized Crime and Terrorism," excerpted in *Trends in Organized Crime*, vol. 3, no. 1 (1997), pp. 85, 90. The report also asserted, in considerable tension with the finding cited in the text, that "Our findings suggest that the total number of criminal cases involving encryption worldwide is at least 500, with an annual growth rate of 50 to 100 percent" and "quite a few people are technically sophisticated."

3. David Kahn, *The Codebreakers* (New York: Scribner, 1996).

4. Ibid., at 395–403.

5. Ibid., at 75.

6. See ⟨http://www.clark.net/pub/cme/html/rump96.html⟩ for details.

7. Carl Ellison, "Establishing Identity Without Certification Authorities," 6th USENIX Security Symposium, San Jose, July 1996, ⟨http://www.clark.net/pub/cme/usenix.html⟩.

PART III

CONTROLLING THE FLOW OF CAPITAL

# 8. Effects of the Regulatory Suppression of Digital Cash

*Eric Hughes*

The flow of money across borders either in the form of large amounts of capital or micropayments for online services is a natural and essential component of global trade. And the movement of money out of jurisdictions with high taxes or restrictions on investment, production, or consumption exerts a powerful disciplinary force on governments. The instantaneous movement of digital money thus holds particular promise for an explosion of global free trade and evolution away from inefficient and unnecessary regulations and forms of taxation.

This essay is about a particular kind of digital money called digital cash. Digital cash is money as a means of payment, not money as a store of value or a unit of account. Like real cash, the payment is anonymous and leaves no accounting trail for law enforcement to follow. Regulatory suppression of digital cash, therefore, is a given.

The digital cash systems in existence to date have been too small to have any impact,[1] so the government has taken no action against them. But this situation reflects the primitive state of the digital cash systems, rather than signifying the systems' compatibility with U.S. regulation. The goal of financial reporting laws is the conversion of the entire financial transaction capacity of the country into a monitoring system for the exertion of the police power. Digital cash, by design, thwarts the efficacy of any such monitoring system. This fact in itself is sufficient to induce suppression. This essay explores how the world's financial infrastructure will lose by failure to embrace digital cash.

The suppression of digital cash will slow the advancement of self-regulation of financial institutions and impede the development of electronic commerce more generally. Digital cash exhibits in overt

Eric Hughes is the chief technology officer and cofounder of Simple Access, Inc.

and obvious form many severe problems latent in other systems. Solving the problems with digital cash would have general benefits across many types of payment systems. Many individually tailored solutions to problems throughout the payment system cannot be as efficient in the aggregate as a single standard solution. The effect of digital cash suppression will be the societal loss of ways of addressing problems whose generic solution portends greater welfare for all.

## Parallels with Encryption

The suppression of digital cash will parallel law enforcement efforts to deter the widespread deployment of encryption. Digital cash makes financial monitoring useless in exactly the same way that encryption makes network monitoring useless. Both technologies devalue the strategy of broad monitoring to worthlessness. However, the laws that enable the suppression of digital cash are somewhat better established than the laws that purport to control encryption. In the case of digital cash, the existing regulatory nexus of the currency and banking systems suffices to prevent a digital cash system from being linked into the dollar system, at least in the United States. Unlike digital cash, however, no such existing nexus exists for communication infrastructure and encryption; indeed, the use of encryption should be protected by the First Amendment. The limit of the current Administration's ability to suppress encryption is the perversion of arms-trafficking regulations against civilian production of cryptographic software for consumer and business markets. Further laws against encryption have not been passed. But legislation intruding on the privacy of financial transactions is well entrenched, beginning with the Bank Secrecy Act. The government has given no indication that it intends to stand down from its monitoring goals. Observers should fully expect, at least in the medium term, the suppression of digital cash in the United States.[2]

## The Nature of Digital Cash

As noted above, digital cash is digital money used as a means of payment. Digital cash allows the bearer to transfer existing value from account to account, not to create *de novo* stores of value. (New stores of value, or synthetic currencies, are also called digital money. Synthetic currencies are money just as specie currencies and fiat currencies are.)

Digital cash is bearer promissory notes issued in digital form by an issuer. The issuer has two functional roles, one as the maker of notes and one as the transfer agent who moves value between the parties to the transaction. One may think of the transfer agent as a bank, but there is no practical or legal requirement that the transfer agent actually be a bank. In the United States, for example, regulations require that the issuer be a bank only if the transfer of value (*not* the transfer of the digital bearer note) passes through a demand deposit account. Digital cash issuers, though, would be considered money transmitters for the purposes of transaction reporting rules.

Digital cash in operation works as follows: The issuer makes a note and transfers it to a purchaser (of the note). Upon issuance, the issuer makes a credit to a suspension account and a debit for the value received for the note; for a bank, that might be a debit to a deposit account. The suspension account is a liability account representing notes outstanding that have not yet been redeemed. When the note has been issued, the purchaser transfers the note to a redeemer to repay a debt or to purchase a service. The redeemer then seeks value for the note from the issuer. Once the issuer has determined that the note remains valid, the issuer gives value for the note. On the books of the issuer, the redemption of the note is entered as a debit to the suspension account and a credit to the account of the redeemer for value given.

The distinctive element of digital cash systems is that the initial debit for value received and the subsequent credit for value given are not linked; they are not entered in the journal as part of the same transaction. The operation of digital cash, therefore, destroys information about the identities of the transacting counterparties. The active and intentional refusal by the issuer to create linkages between counterparties is the defining characteristic of digital cash. Digital cash acts like cash; the instrument itself has no history and creates no audit trail.

The benefits of digital cash parallel the benefits of real cash; it preserves privacy for the buyer of goods and enables the seller to secure payment at very low cost. For vast numbers of transactions, the seller of goods has no reason to care who the buyer is, as long as he is paid. Once he is paid, the transaction is over. Given the number of economic transactions that occur every day in the economy, instruments that require the seller to identify the buyer and store the identity or other information waste time and resources. This waste factor is multiplied a hundred- or a thousandfold by electronic commerce, which enables far more transactions to take place in a given period of time. Digital cash would enable billions of microtransactions (pay $.05 to download this photo!) that otherwise could not exist.

Also, the difficulty of tracing cash (either digital or real) ensures that money will remain fungible by cutting off later claimants to the money, the cash equivalent of a *bona fide* purchaser without notice. Imagine an economic system in which, if I accepted payment from a buyer, a later claimant (say, Suzy) could come along and claim the money from me on the grounds that the buyer received the money in change by a grocer, who received it from Johnny who had stolen it from Suzy. The entire economy would be paralyzed by fear that property rights in goods and money could never be established.

Similar electronic payment systems that do not preserve anonymity are not correctly described as digital cash. One variety of note-based payment system offers counterparty anonymity but not issuer anonymity. Properly speaking, it is a digital note system, a class that includes a digital cash system but is not identical with it. Some smart-card systems, such as Mondex, do not use instrument-based transfer. These are encrypted balance systems, which protect a remote ledger entry from improper modification. Mondex offers counterparty anonymity, but the devices log transactions internally and the system offers little anonymity against the issuer.

### The Self-Hazard of Digital Cash

The central risk that digital cash creates for the organizations that use it is self-hazard, typically, embezzlement. Digital cash, by design, removes the possibility of tracking money. Employees of a company with signature authority over assets can convert them to digital cash and either flee or avoid internal auditing. Thus, any company that makes payments using digital cash incurs embezzlement risk, just as any business that deals with large amounts of physical cash does. At the very top of the list of businesses with exposure to this risk is the issuer itself. A truly successful digital cash system is a first-class threat to the originator of the system.

Current digital cash systems are miniscule; thus, they would not effectively shield embezzlement. A small system simply does not provide a sufficient conduit for digital funds nor a wide enough shield against identification. This principle, however, has a counter-intuitive and dangerous converse. Every system fielded will appear safe until some point in its growth at which it rapidly becomes unsafe. Given the lock-in effects of adoption of systems requiring compatibility, and payment systems certainly do, such a system becomes unsafe precisely at the moment it becomes indispensable.

One solution would be to treat digital cash as petty cash, with similar procedures. For petty cash, rules that restrict daily transaction volumes suffice to bound the risk low enough to prevent flight. Other prevailing ways of addressing the problem of self-hazard rely upon identification, record-keeping, and recovery.

But that kind of change cannot work for businesses with extensive involvement with digital cash. The methods focus more on the eventual correction of a failure than on prevention. After-the-fact actions can do little good against the particular hazards presented by digital cash, so new techniques that focus more on prevention must arise.

The new techniques would have widespread implications for improving security and certainty of many other transactions. The core of the self-hazard problem arises out of the classic dilemma of how to ensure that an agent acts in the best interests of the principal. The principal-agent relationship is ubiquitous in commerce. Since any solution to the self-hazard problem must alter the nature of the customary relationship between principal and agent, each such solution has a wide area of potential application.

In the case of digital cash, the principals are the joint owners of the issuing company. The agents are officers and employees of the company. The company has assets under the fiduciary discretion of the officers. The delay between an action by an agent of the company and an accounting for that action provides the time gap whence comes the opportunity for malfeasance. Discretion and an interval of opportunity combine to make the hazard.

A related hazard surrounds the viability of the issuer as a trusted intermediary. Here the principal-agent relationship per se is not at issue, but rather the fiduciary trustworthiness of the issuer is. The value given for digital notes sits in some suspension fund. The issuer holds the funds in trust for the bearers of the notes and might abscond with the money. The issuer must therefore convince prospective customers that the possibility is not a potentiality. Presumably success in persuasion requires the issuer to have effective controls in place against the possibility.

## Limited Agency and Narrow Function

The remedy to the self-hazards is to restrict the discretion of the agent. The principal-agent relationship has always countenanced limited agency. What is new, however, is the creation of an agency system that concentrates on prior restrictions in a fast-moving digital environment.

In many situations of limited agency, the principal may achieve greater reliability by associating limitations to agency with some artifact (e.g., a bank account). The inherent limitations on the artifact supplement the restrictions on the agent proper. Creating such an artifact of narrow function is a key part of limiting the agent.

Another important piece of the puzzle in reducing the self-hazard of digital cash is to ensure that the document authorizing the agent to act on behalf of the principal is communicated by the principal, not by the agent. Because of the impossibility of correcting a digital cash transaction, self-representation by an agent is insufficient. Digital cash requires software compatibility and the establishment of a communication channel for principals to declare and announce their agents.

The communication channel also will enable the issuer to establish internal and external controls on the agent. An internal control affects messages that never leave the organization; an external control involves an outside party. Simply delegating a role in the transaction to an outside party can create external control. For example, the ability to grant authorization to trade on an account requires the cooperation of the brokerage making the account. Internal agency controls operate by dividing the organization into components that must deal with each other as if they were external parties. The instantaneous nature of digital cash and digital communications will allow organizations easily to involve a neutral third party in a transaction to control the agent. In essence, outside cooperation converts internal controls into external controls.

A company can prevent the most obvious types of embezzlement by implementing an internal restriction against self-dealing and dividing responsibility for assets and liabilities within the company. The restriction is not sufficient by itself, as the organization must prevent funds from being looped through other institutions. The second layer of protection involves external controls. One implication of this is that all the correspondents of an issuer must also participate in the agency system. In other words, the agency system must be pervasive for digital cash not to be a self-hazard.

## Bankruptcy and Narrow Books

If limited agency presents a single principle for solving problems around discretion, there always remains a residue of risk that the agency system will fail and bankruptcy ensue. In this case, the owners of the issuer are responsible for this and should bear the loss. But in bankruptcy, other parties will lose as well. By assumption, a successful system has a large reserve in suspension accounts that fund unredeemed notes.[3] The issuer has a legal liability to repay, but that liability is moot if the issuer is insolvent and goes into default. Note holders, therefore, bear a nonrecourse risk that their digital notes will become bogus money.

Bankruptcy rules can mitigate the default risk to note holders. Rules honoring partitioned accounts can protect note holders against issuer failure. The principle of account partitioning allows the splitting of the assets and liabilities of the organization into multiple books. A single book—the wide book—describes the company's own assets and liabilities. One or more other narrow books represent operations like digital cash issuance where the assets are essentially held in trust for the liability account holders.

Today there is but a single wide book (in this sense) for an entire company. In bankruptcy, all the assets of the single book are available, under a set of priority rules, to claimants. In a narrow books bankruptcy model, the assets of a narrow book are reserved entirely for the discharge of the liabilities of that book. For example, imagine a digital cash issuer with one wide book and only one narrow book for note issuance. If the wide book goes into default, the note holders may redeem their notes out of the assets of the narrow book. Further digital cash issuance would cease, but the notes would not become bogus. If the narrow book went into default, the issuer would perform a mandatory transfer of assets from the wide book to the narrow book to cover the shortfall. In other words, failure can propagate inward from narrow to wide but not outward from general liabilities to specific ones.

Narrow book accounting helps prove the viability of the issuer to a potential user of their notes. The narrow book, with its highly restricted set of possible activities, makes possible a higher degree of assurance about the reliability of the agency mechanism. The division also reduces the incentives to a criminal, as with fewer assets available to any single effort at theft, the net gain from criminal activity is correspondingly reduced.

The narrow book is similar in spirit to the narrow bank. Indeed, if it becomes possible to implement narrow books, it will be possible to implement a narrow bank as an accounting structure rather than as a separate entity. The principle herein generalizes to every kind of financial intermediation. When an intermediary acts on behalf of a client, the activity can take place in some suitably partitioned narrow book. The activity may be asset holding, investment, funds transfer, trading, and so forth. For some applications, the partition boundary may travel right down to the level of the individual account holder. In this situation, the narrow book enables the equivalent of an individually insured deposit account.

Narrow book accounting also provides an avenue for the securitization of commercial banking activities. A bank puts assets it wishes to securitize into a narrow book and limits agency for those assets to make them immovable. The bank sells off the assets by entering liabilities in the narrow book. The combination of the narrow book and the limitations on transfer of assets effectively re-create a security. The existing account infrastructure of the bank becomes the registrar and transfer agent. Trading and pricing can occur elsewhere. The key is that the enforced removal of discretion over the assets makes it possible to treat an asset as a security.

### Real-Time Auditing

Limited agency represents a necessary prevention mechanism, but assurance that the mechanisms are actually preventing failure requires detection mechanisms. Internal detection mechanisms alone cannot provide an independent assurance of solvency, giving rise to the need for auditing. Assuming that a failure in the agency system does occur, the speed of detection determines the maximum exposure to loss. As the speed of transaction increases, daily reconciliation will no longer be fast enough to catch errors in time. Indeed, the reconciliation process must begin to operate in tandem with each transaction. The auditing requirement is to verify solvency. Continuous reconciliation gives rise to real-time auditing.

The solvency requirements are independent of the agency system. Agency restrictions can prevent a transaction from completing because of a lack of authorization. Solvency requirements embodied in a real-time auditing system can prevent a transaction from completing because doing so would create insolvency. More concretely, an officer cannot simply transfer funds out of suspension accounts because there is no authorization to do so, but even if the officer gained authorization (presumably incorrectly) the transaction could not complete, because the result would be insufficient covering funds for unpaid notes. Real-time auditing creates a second layer of protection of the viability of a digital cash issuer.

Assurance of solvency must directly involve the books of the issuer and the corresponding entries in counterparty books. An asset on the books of an issuer corresponds to a liability on the counterparty books, and misrepresentation might occur. The auditing system that provides full assurances of solvency therefore will rely on a system of communications in the same way that a system of limited agency does.

Real-time auditing comes into its own in combination with narrow book accounting in bankruptcy. The bankruptcy rules assure a proper partitioning of assets; real-time auditing assures that the assets retain their value no matter when bankruptcy occurs. Real-time auditing also promotes the treatment of certain books as a securities registry. The agency system may ensure that the narrow book is supposed to have the right properties, but the real-time audit guarantees that it does.

## De Facto Anonymity

Each of the techniques described to prevent self-hazard in digital cash—limited agency, narrow function, externalization of limited agency, narrow books, bankruptcy partitioning, real-time auditing, solvency requirements—is applicable to digital cash systems. But the measures described are effective in any environment in which recourse is limited by circumstance. With digital cash, recourse is limited by anonymity and by transaction speed. Other circumstances, however, equally effectively limit recourse. The methods evolved to reduce the risk of dealing in digital cash have wide application to those situations.

De facto anonymity is the effective absence of real identity in a transaction. In this situation, the limitation on recourse is not one of impossibility, as with digital cash, but one of unfeasibility. Even in possession of a true identity, de facto anonymity can arise in several ways. The cost of pursuing a claim may be high, particularly if a change of jurisdiction is involved. The value of the transaction may be low and not worth pursuing. The cost of recovery of assets after judgment may be high. In each case, using one's knowledge of the debtor's name to pursue him or her has an absolute disadvantage over accepting the loss. In other situations, though, use of the name may also be at a comparative disadvantage relative to other activities the company might pursue. Either way, techniques that work with digital cash certainly apply to situations of de facto anonymity.

As uncomfortable as it may seem, de facto anonymity is an insepa-rable part of commercial interactions. The faster networks, higher transaction volumes, and lower transaction amounts enabled by digital cash and electronic networks simply exacerbate the problem. In every case in which recourse is possible but not economical, one may treat the situation identically as if recourse were in fact impossible.

Broadly speaking, mechanisms to control hazard operate either before the fact or after the fact, either forward or rearward. The lesson of digital cash is that it is possible to design a system that uses only forward mechanisms. Stable systems need not rely upon rearward mechanisms.

The fathers of all rearward mechanisms are prosecution and incar-ceration. Historically speaking, it may well have been more economi-cal for society to externalize the costs of bad security onto the govern-ment than to implement good enough security. I will leave that issue for policy historians to discuss. What is clear today, however, is that forward mechanisms can be inexpensive enough that externalizing criminal-making expenses to the government will no longer be to the benefit of society. There is no excuse, with the cost of computation so low and with the capability of distributed systems to prevent single-point failure so robust. The choice is not whether to pick between forward and rearward mechanisms, but to choose between a system of mixed forward and rearward mechanisms on one hand, and on the other a system of forward mechanisms only.

Nevertheless, it is not obvious that there is sufficient incentive for any single party to develop or to deploy forward mechanisms initially. With vigorous efforts to suppress digital cash and all similar systems that create real anonymity, no system requires the evolution of a system controlled by forward mechanisms alone. While other systems obviously may benefit from forward mechanisms, it is frequently cheaper to rely upon identification and prosecution. Exactly because the forward solutions from digital cash are systems of communication and compatibility, they have high barriers to single-party entry. Any single party wishing to pursue limited agency, for example, needs to convince cooperative neighbors to incur a cost in their own organizations so that the system of limited agency might be efficacious. This multiparty bootstrapping hurdle is enormous and is almost never overcome except by necessity.

Even if advanced forward mechanisms can be deployed, the objection may arise that lack of the deterrence from rearward mechanisms will induce a criminal class to pursue criminal activity. Perhaps this might be true if the forward mechanisms did not work better, but suppose, for the sake of discussion, that both approaches worked equally well. Getting away with a crime when the downside risk is confrontation with authority is far different than getting away with a crime when the downside is hours of boredom. I posit that there will be less crime when criminal activity usually does not work and is boring, rather than when it usually does not work but may have adrenaline-rousing consequences.

Forward mechanisms are hardly uncommon in finance. One of the most venerable instruments of banking, the letter of credit, is exactly a solution to de facto anonymity. The LC originated in international trade, where the effective distance between parties was far larger than today. The LC is a proxy substitution of credit that relies upon existing banking relationships for its integrity. The principle of advance protection is already well established in financial systems. What remains is to methodically replace the remaining rearward mechanisms with forward ones.

After all the arguments about technical merit have concluded, the choice of mechanisms is also cultural. Rearward mechanisms necessarily entail a regime of identification, dossiers, police, prison, courts, and lawyers. The cost of supporting this overhead is the externalized cost of systemic absence of sufficiently robust forward mechanisms. Even when faced with the availability of adequate forward mechanisms, many people may prefer this regime. It has worked in the past and it is proven. The conservative choice is to keep the *status quo*, and prosecution and other rearward mechanisms are certainly the *status quo*.

The alternative is responsibility for one's own protection. The nature of a system of limited agency ensures that one cannot protect oneself in this way without the cooperation of peers. The forward mechanisms described here may be seen as the substitution of trusted people with interlocking incentives. Rather than a threat to cooperate, forward mechanisms create an inducement to cooperate. The approach which abnegates prosecution is, thus speaking, a market-based approach.

Hence the essential difference between the two mindsets is not one between cooperation and violence. Rather, in both kinds of structures the parties involved cooperate. The difference is in the nature of the cooperation. The system that includes rearward mechanisms is one that cooperates through the principle of a sovereign—the state—that has the power to punish. The system that denies rearward mechanisms cooperates through the principle of the market—mutual assistance, with settlements—that has the power to persuade and exhort. In the end, the effect of the suppression of digital cash is the suppression of the culture of the market in favor of the culture of the sovereign.

## Notes

1. Andrea McKenna Findlay, "Pence, Not Pennies, Go Online," *Financial Services Online*, September, 1998, pp. 1–3 (describing the obstacles to consumer enthusiasm for digital money in the United States); David C. Stewart, "Picking Winners and Losers in Digital Cash," *Bank Technology News*, October 1997, p. 1 (comparing different digital cash products in detail).

2. While few concrete regulatory proposals are forthcoming, a slew of articles describes regulators' unease about digital cash. Vary Coats and Steve Bonorris, "Digital Money: Electronic Cash May Make Sense," *The Futurist*, August 18, 1998, p. 22 (reporting concern about digital cash at the Internal Revenue Service, the Federal Reserve System, and among other regulatory and law enforcement authorities, but noting that "So far, the U.S. government has adopted a hands-off, wait-and-see position on digital money. Federal Reserve Chairman Alan Greenspan says that premature regulation could either stifle innovation or create monetary instruments that neither consumers nor merchants want"); "EU To Launch Scheme on Credit Card Payment," *Businessworld*, August 4, 1998, p. 1 (describing European Commission

proposals to regulate electronic payment cards issued by nonbanks); Malcolm McDonald, "IRD Faces Tough Questions on Net Taxes," *The Dominion,* April 6, 1998, p. 4; "Digital Cash May Increase Money Laundering," *Private Banker International,* March, 1998, p. 12; Sougata Mukherjee, "Digital Cash Intensifies Money Laundering Fears," *Washington Business Journal,* February 13, 1998, p. 8 (discussing a report issued by the Institute of Technology Assessment calling for immediate regulatory action to combat the use of digital cash in money laundering); Adam Courtenay, "The Sky's the Limit: The Information Superhighway Is Presenting New Opportunities for Money Laundering and Tax Evasion," *The Banker,* February, 1998, p. 52 (describing concerns of many regulatory agencies); Douglas Hayward, "Digital Money: Stimulus for New Types of Commerce," *Financial Times (London),* January 7, 1998, p. 15 (quoting Stanley Morris, director of the U.S. Treasury's Financial Crimes Enforcement Network, as saying, "Depending how it evolves, digital cash has the potential to increase the power to launder money or evade taxes. . . . The fact is that change creates new vulnerabilities, and we want to head those off at the pass.").

3. I am assuming a 100 percent reserves system here. If the issuer is practicing fractional reserve issuance, it can be viable only if other assets are available to back the note issuance, even if illiquid. In either case the issuer has open liabilities in the total amount in suspension. The liability holders, that is, the note holders, also bear risk for bankruptcy failure.

# 9. America the Financial Imperialist

### Richard W. Rahn

*America is a large friendly dog in a very small room.*
*Every time it wags its tail it knocks over a chair.*

*Arnold Toynbee*

If something is illegal in the United States, many Americans think it ought to be illegal everywhere. And likewise, if something is legal in the United States, Americans think it ought to be legal everywhere. The problem with this world view is that it is not shared by much of the rest of the world's people.

American law is largely an outgrowth of the English common law, and hence most of those countries that England once ruled have a somewhat similar approach to the law. Much of continental Europe, on the other hand, has a legal system derived from the Napoleonic code. Many of the Moslem countries have systems based on Islamic law, which, for example, prohibits the payment of interest.

While all societies have strict rules against murder and theft, some activities are serious crimes in some countries but not in others. Many environmental crimes are unknown in the former communist countries and the third world. Whether prostitution, pot smoking, adultery, public nudity at the beach, or slander is a crime depends on where one is. The same is true with financial crimes. For example, there are very different attitudes among societies toward tax evasion, money laundering, bribe taking, and nepotism.

Most countries have a territorial system of taxation, whereby a person only pays tax on the money earned in that particular country. The United States has a worldwide tax system, in which citizens and permanent U.S. residents are taxed on their worldwide income.

Richard W. Rahn is president and CEO of Novecon, and is the author of a new book, *The End of Money and the Struggle for Financial Privacy*, from which portions of this chapter are excerpted.

Most countries do not have a capital gains tax, at least not a broad one like the United States.

These real differences cause serious conflict. This is particularly true when the United States tries to apply its laws outside the territory of the United States—especially when the activity is not illegal in the foreign country.

U.S. authorities often inspect people's bank accounts wherever the account might be. In fact, some U.S. officials at times even have tried to look in foreign bank accounts of non-U.S. citizens. Many countries look at such behavior as unseemly and immoral. A number of countries have passed real bank privacy laws, unlike the U.S. (anti-) Bank Secrecy Act, to prohibit either private bank officials or government officials from looking into private bank accounts. In contrast, U.S. officials have been known to pressure foreign governments and bankers to look at private accounts. The requests often generate considerable friction, particularly when the Internal Revenue Service (IRS) or Federal Bureau of Investigation (FBI) demands that foreign officials violate their own laws. For example, Swiss bank privacy does not apply to accounts where the money is believed to have come from criminal sources. However, tax avoidance is not considered a criminal offense in Switzerland, and hence the veil of bank privacy will not be removed for the IRS.

U.S. bank regulatory authorities are insistent on requiring banks to "know their customers." The regulation is imposed on foreign banks doing business in the United States as well as U.S. banks operating in foreign countries, and the regulation is not limited to accounts in the banks in the United States. Many people like to hold their bank accounts in the name of a separate entity for privacy and protection. It is common for wealthy South Americans to set up bank accounts in offshore branches of large international banks in the name of their personal investment company, rather than their own name, as a shield against kidnapping. To protect their citizens, a number of South American countries make it illegal for a bank to reveal the name of the beneficial owner. But U.S. authorities often demand to know the real owners of these accounts. The international banks are then put in the impossible situation of being unable to comply with the conflicting laws of two different countries.

According to U.S. law, foreign banks operating in the United States are supposed to be treated by the regulatory authorities exactly the same as the U.S. banks. Yet bank executives of foreign banks operating in the United States find that this is not always the case. Some U.S. government regulatory officials are so ignorant they assume that anyone who has an account in a foreign bank—particularly a bank whose home country has bank privacy laws, such as Switzerland—must be engaged in criminal activities. As a result, they treat responsible and highly professional bank executives working for foreign banks as if they work for dishonorable organizations. It appears never to have occurred to the U.S. officials that Americans and others might wish to have accounts in foreign-owned banks because they get better or a wider range of services than they get from U.S.-owned banks.[1]

Most Americans, and especially American business people, like the fact that U.S. banks operate in many foreign countries. It serves their American customers well. If Americans want U.S. banks to have the right to operate in foreign countries and not be discriminated against, then they need to extend the same privileges and courtesies to foreign-owned banks operating in the United States.

There are endless examples of abusive and improper behavior by U.S. officials against foreign bankers and citizens. For instance, the *Journal of Commerce* notes, "In a case involving Marine Midland Bank, prosecutors froze $7 million in the correspondent account of the Hong Kong and Shanghai Bank in Panama, even though they were only looking for $1.5 million in dirty money."[2] In another example, "Bank Leu SA of Luxembourg forfeited $2.3 million to the U.S. government and more than $1 million to Luxembourg following a money-laundering guilty plea in San Francisco, even though Bank Leu had no branch in the United States. The charge? Clearing U.S. dollars drawn on a U.S. bank but deposited by non-U.S. citizens in Luxembourg."[3] If any foreign country had treated U.S. citizens and banks in a similar manner, there would have been screams of outrage. U.S. politicians and authorities would have demanded sanctions. This hypocrisy blemishes the reputations of all Americans.

## Excessive Costs of Compliance with Worthless Regulations

The regulations and reporting requirements imposed by the U.S. government on financial institutions not only violate Americans' civil liberties, but fail the most elementary tests of costs and benefits. Senior bank compliance executives estimate that approximately 15 to 20 percent of bank operating costs in the United States are due to the costs of trying to comply with federal money laws and regulations. The reason the cost is so high is that almost all bank employees have to be trained and monitored to make sure they are adequately spying on their customers. Each transaction has to be evaluated and any transaction involving large amounts of money or cash in excess of $3,000 must be reported.

Government does not make the task any easier. The forms that are submitted to the government must be typed, though most banks no longer use typewriters, they use computers. The bank compliance officer of one of the world's largest banks said that when he asked if they could supply the reports in electronic format, he was given the software for the forms from the bank regulators. However, when he tried to submit the reports using the software he had been given by the government, he was told that the regulations still required him to submit individual typed reports.[4]

The costs are, of course, passed on to the banks' customers. In essence, Americans are paying billions of dollars each year in hidden federal taxes on their financial operations. What do they get for this "tax," besides a massive invasion into their financial privacy? Not much!

In the 10-year period from 1987–96, banks filed more than 77 million Currency Transactions Reports (CTRs) with the U.S. Treasury. That amounts to approximately 308,000 pounds of paper.[5] Those are reports on transactions over $3,000 that must be filed by bank employees. Such reports caused the government to file about 3,000 money laundering cases between 1987 and 1995. A total of 7,300 defendants were charged but only 580 people were convicted, according to the Justice Department.[6] Environmentalists take note: this works out to about 531 pounds of paper per conviction.

The government often runs sting operations in luxurious Caribbean locations. Such operations are great for scenes in movies, but in reality most of them are a big bust financed by the taxpayer. Of the 290 people charged as a result of the bank sting operations between 1990 and 1995, only 29 were found guilty.[7] As wasteful as is the financial cost to the taxpayer for so few convictions, the real tragedy is the cost to all of those innocent people who had huge legal expenses and often their lives ruined because of incompetent and, in some cases, over-zealous government prosecutors.

There is no evidence that the government anti-money laundering crusade has had any appreciable impact on drug dealing, terrorism, or organized crime. The few convictions that have been obtained are in almost all cases the "small fry." It does not take a criminal genius to figure out how to get around the U.S. government reporting requirements and to launder money, and the big guys can afford to hire all the lawyers and others to take care of the problem for them. In addition, according to former Federal Reserve Board governor Lawrence Lindsey, the money laundering laws discriminate against the poor. The poor are the least likely to have established relationships with banks and the most likely to operate primarily with cash. Hence, they are the first to be targeted, and this even further discourages bankers from wanting their business.

Anyone willing to devote a little intelligence, time, and effort to laundering money can now do so, and will be able to under almost any conceivable regulation with only a minuscule chance of being convicted. The real total cost for each money laundering conviction per year appears to be over $100 million—an obscene waste of money. The costs to the banks run in the tens of billions of dollars; the costs of the federal government enforcement efforts run into the low billions of dollars. The costs result in higher bank charges, higher taxes, and lower quality financial services for Americans. If the money laundering war was a shooting war, and if it cost $100 million or even $1 million for each enemy fatality, the United States would have been bankrupted after its first major battle. Or to look at it in another way, if the real total cost of the war on money laundering is only $10 billion, it is roughly equal to what the federal government spends on child nutrition programs. Other law enforcement surely could spend money to better effect.

Members of Congress and others have attacked Judge Kenneth Starr and other "special prosecutors" for the cost of each conviction, yet their costs of conviction are a small fraction of the real cost of conviction of each money launderer.

The government financial regulators will claim that, even though they cannot justify the costs they impose on an expense-to-conviction basis, their activities have a big deterrent effect. They will provide data to show that when they target a particular geographical area, the number of currency wire transfers declines. In reality, people merely move their activity to a different location once the targeting orders are announced. The effect is equivalent to squeezing a balloon.

By any fair, objective standard, the war on money laundering has been a colossal failure. It has not hurt drug dealers, terrorists, or assorted criminals. It has hurt the American taxpayer and financial institutions. It has only benefited those in government who owe their jobs to the enforcement effort. The war on money laundering has in reality been a war on the pocketbooks and civil liberties of the American people, carried out by government bureaucrats.

## Notes

1. Examples of such behavior were given to me by senior officers of Swiss banks operating in the United States. For obvious reasons, they have chosen to remain anonymous.

2. "Clean Getaway for Money Launderers," *Journal of Commerce*, December 10, 1996, p. 63.

3. Ibid.

4. From an anonymous interview with a senior bank compliance executive for a major world bank, January 1998.

5. Former Federal Reserve governor Lawrence Lindsey, Cato Institute Debate, "Should Money Laundering Be a Crime?" Cato Institute, Washington, December 5, 1997.

6. "Clean Getaway for Money Launderers," p. 62.

7. Ibid.

PART IV

TRADE SANCTIONS

# 10. Unilateral Sanctions: A Politically Attractive Loser

*Clayton Yeutter*

One of the remarkable, and laudable, qualities of Americans is that we want to make the world a better place. We also want to define just what that term means. For most of the past half century, doing so was relatively simple. We focused our concern on the threat of communism as an ideology, and more specifically on the national security threat posed by the Soviet Union. Those preoccupations have now been moved aside, hopefully forever.

In the aftermath of the cold war, Americans have begun to search for new ways to make the world a better place, but the focus is much more diffuse, much less clear, and far less coherent. We are still behavior oriented, but now our concerns range from nuclear proliferation to drug trafficking, human rights violations, religious persecution, and a whole host of other ills in a myriad of countries. We seem now to be discovering misconduct almost everywhere, and in the inimitable way of Americans we want to do something about it.

Though we are still somewhat perplexed by all this reprehensible behavior, we are not at all perplexed about how to respond. Our weapon of choice is sanctions, and we typically go it alone with unilateral sanctions. We have made ourselves the world's policeman in the post-cold war period, and we have been "assessing fines" in lots of places for lots of offenses. The President's Export Council calculated that, in 1997, more than half the world's people were threatened by U.S. sanctions.

## Asking Hard Questions about Sanctions

We have certainly been sending plenty of "messages" to the rest of the world, and doing so via sanctions is serious business. Whether

Clayton Yeutter is of counsel to the Washington law firm Hogan & Hartson, and the former U.S. secretary of Agriculture and U.S. trade representative.

effective or not, the implementation of unilateral economic sanctions is not likely to be greeted warmly by any recipient nation. Sanctions will inevitably be perceived as an attempt to impose our will, our standards of conduct, our value structure on the other country. And we would not like it one bit if the situation were reversed.

USA*ENGAGE, a consortium of nearly 700 U.S. private-sector entities, has begun to ask some fundamental questions about U.S. sanctions policy:

"Do we really know what we are doing—to ourselves and to others?"

"Is this a carefully considered strategy, or are we shooting from the hip?"

"Have we evaluated the track record of unilateral, or multilateral, sanctions? Have they accomplished their objectives, or did they do more harm than good?"

"Do sanctions have an impact on those responsible for reprehensible behavior, and do they alter that behavior? Or do they hurt a lot of innocent bystanders?"

"Since sanctions almost always take away American jobs, were they worth it? How many jobs were lost, and were they offset by U.S. foreign policy victories?"

"Did they bring about a better world, or did they make things worse?"

"Does the rest of the world have more respect for the United States than before sanctions were imposed? Or less respect?"

If we answer these fundamental questions honestly and objectively, we shall not be pleased with ourselves, and we shall certainly be frustrated. We shall discover that unilateral sanctions are almost always a loser in economic terms, and more often a loser than a winner in foreign policy terms. The track record for multilateral sanctions (where we are joined by our major allies) is better, but not that much better.

So why do we keep doing this? For the simple reason that we have not yet found a better way to express our displeasure with abhorrent behavior, or a better way to alter that behavior. Yet there has to be a better way!

### Personal and Corporate Relations Disrupted

First, some explanation is in order on why unilateral sanctions are unwise. Huge numbers of American jobs are today dependent, partially or wholly, on exports. The jobs are at thousands of firms—small, medium, and large. They are in every state. Nevertheless, our attitude has been, "So what if we have to sacrifice a few jobs when we implement sanctions? There are plenty of other jobs available in this high-powered economy of ours." And so it seems. But nothing goes up forever, and the business cycle has not yet disappeared in America. When we do have a domestic downturn, the policy response will be, "Let's crank up our exports." We will then be looking for eager, enthusiastic foreign buyers, happy to do business with American firms. Will they be there? Or will they say: "We thought you Americans did not want to do business with us"? We could pay a price for the ill will created by U.S. sanctions.

Even more important, we must recognize that *relationships*, personal and corporate, are exceedingly important today in the conduct of international business—and are becoming ever more important. Sanctions inevitably disrupt relationships, but we seem not to be terribly concerned about that. Our attitude is, "So what if we interrupt business between the United States and another country for a year or so? Things will return to normal when those folks straighten out and fly right."

But will they? We announced our intent to embargo soybean exports 25 years ago, and that situation has yet to return to normality. The true cost of economic sanctions is ongoing, typically far beyond the expiration of the sanctions themselves.

We must recognize, too, that the job loss associated with economic sanctions will in the future be greater than it is today. The international relationships I have just mentioned are now becoming much more formalized, in a variety of creative ways. The most recent headline example is the Daimler Benz/Chrysler merger, but there are thousands of other joint ventures, large and small. They range from long-term contractual commitments to cross-border investments, alliances, licensing and other marketing agreements, and a host of others. In some instances the relationships have led to formation of a "team" that functions all the way from producer to consumer within a particular industry.

How is an American firm to be accepted as a team member if its representative says, "I am sorry to tell you this, but because of U.S. economic sanctions programs, we will not be able to do business in countries A, B, C and . . . "? Guess who will be dumped from the team rather quickly and not be invited back.

The fundamental point being made by USA*ENGAGE is that we ought to stop and think before we impose economic sanctions. And we ought to compare the expected benefits, in foreign policy and other terms (including moral leadership), with the expected costs, in economic and other terms (including damaged relationships).

We are most likely underestimating the cost of unilateral sanctions, especially in the long term. And I expect we are grossly underestimating them.

## Give Diplomacy a Chance

Is there a better way? Of course. Our initial effort in dealing with deplorable conduct ought to be through good old-fashioned diplomacy. That has less political appeal than sanctions, of course, because diplomacy often moves slowly. We Americans want a rapid-fire, decisive response from our political leaders in such situations. And our political leaders seek to provide such a response, often knowing full well that it will not succeed! After all, it is difficult to get an unruly teenager to change behavior overnight, let alone the government of a nation. We need to exercise some emotional restraint in these situations, give diplomacy a chance, and hold our diplomats accountable for how they handle, or mishandle, such situations. Today we rush decisively, but precipitously, to sanctions, and our diplomats become nonplayers in the process. They are not given a chance to demonstrate their wares and prove their worth.

Do our diplomats have sufficient leverage, outside the realm of economic sanctions, to alter such reprehensible behavior? Not always, of course, but we should not underestimate the diplomatic power and prowess at our command. One can conjure lots of ways to make an irresponsible government squirm, including massive global exposure of its transgressions. Our diplomats should have no difficulty developing a long list of "leverage points."

But there will be times when a government is intransigent and diplomacy will fail, or its conduct is so reprehensible that a delayed response would be unconscionable. In either of those situations, our model should be the Gulf War coalition pulled together so skillfully by President Bush several years ago. That takes work, for coalitions do not come together automatically, for any purpose. The easy way is to go it alone, through unilateral sanctions, and that is what we have been inclined to do. But it is the wrong way, for it is almost always doomed to fail. Let us expend the energy and the intellectual horsepower to do it the right way, through multilateral sanctions. Then we will have at least a reasonable chance of success.

Does all this mean we should never implement unilateral economic sanctions? Not at all, for sometimes diplomacy will fail or we will not be able to generate the support of our allies. We are then left with the option of doing nothing or using unilateral sanctions. We will sometimes choose the former, for we cannot rectify every transgression in the world. Sometimes we will choose the latter (hopefully as a *last* resort, rather than a *first* resort), even though sanctions may "hurt us more than they do the other guy."

But let us have some flexibility in sanctions legislation. The sanctions laws now on our books are too rigid. They constitute foreign policy by fiat, and the world is far too complex and fast-moving for any country to conduct its foreign policy in that manner. This inflexibility leads either to the incongruous implementation of unilateral sanctions, or to establishing an incongruous rationale for not implementing them. Either way, we look foolish.

Let us make sure unilateral sanctions are the exception rather than the rule in dealing with deplorable conduct in other nations. And let us make sure the implementation of sanctions is a considered decision, made after careful calculation of the probable costs and benefits. In a nutshell, let us stop taking wild swings with unilateral economic sanctions. We have been hitting ourselves in the chin far too often.

# 11. Economic Sanctions: America's Folly
## Gary C. Hufbauer

President Woodrow Wilson sparked America's love affair with economic sanctions. After the carnage of the First World War, Wilson proclaimed:

> A nation boycotted is a nation that is in sight of surrender. Apply this economic, peaceful, silent, deadly remedy, and there will be no need for force. It is a terrible remedy. It does not cost a life outside the nation boycotted, but it brings pressure upon the nation that, in my judgment, no modern nation could resist.

America has tempered much else in the Wilsonian vision. We do not expect the United Nations to broker disputes between great powers. We do not champion an independent state for each ethnic nationality. We do not elevate democracy above all other interests.

### The Grand Experiment

But when it comes to economic sanctions, we not only embrace the Wilsonian vision, we embellish upon it. In fact, we use sanctions so often—nearly 100 times this century—that they have become America's grand diplomatic experiment. This experiment, repeated many times, shows that three of Wilson's assertions, seemingly self-evident when declared at Indianapolis in 1919, are quite often and quite simply wrong:

- A nation boycotted is not in sight of surrender: recall North Korea, Cuba, and Iran.
- In achieving "high" foreign policy goals, sanctions are not a substitute for force, but they can be a prelude to force—consider Iraq, Haiti, and Bosnia.

Gary C. Hufbauer is a senior fellow at the Institute for International Economics.

- Contrary to Wilson's belief, economic sanctions have turned out to be an offer that nearly every target can refuse—not only powerful China, but also powerless Panama.

In the face of this doubtful record, Presidents Jimmy Carter, Ronald Reagan, George Bush, and Bill Clinton nevertheless embraced economic sanctions as a major instrument in the U.S. diplomatic repertoire. Indeed, in the post-cold war era, sanctions have become the lead violin of American foreign policy. The federal government now imposes sanctions, small and large, against at least 40 countries; joining in the diplomatic laboratory, state and municipal governments have enacted some 25 sanctions in the last two years, and another 16 are pending. The most recent sanctions are directed not only against adversaries but conspicuously against our allies.

The conventional rationale for America's folly is straightforward: as the superpower standing astride the global economy, the United States has a special responsibility to deal with misdeeds and despots in many places. Military force is too costly and customary diplomacy is too feeble. Economic sanctions must therefore be applied like a global salve, liberally to every wound.

Lurking behind the conventional rationale are pragmatic reasons that too often come into play: congressmen, governors, and mayors who sponsor sanctions can reap all the political thrill of playing "Secretary of State for a Day" without bearing any of the responsibility. The grievances of religious and ethnic minorities at home can be answered (and their votes acquired) by dishing our punishment to governments abroad.

## Consequences of the Grand Experiment

"Seward's Folly" would have had no great consequence, even if the Alaska purchase had turned out a great boondoggle instead of a great bonanza. All that would have been lost was $15 million. The same insignificance cannot be attributed to the nation's grand experiment with economic sanctions. President Wilson was right on one key point, if not for the reasons he imagined. Sanctions are a "terrible remedy."

Economic sanctions today cost the United States some $15 billion to $20 billion in lost exports, depriving American workers of some 200,000 well-paid jobs. It would be one thing if the costs were compensated from the public purse, so that everyone shared the burden;

it is quite another when the costs are concentrated episodically on individual firms and communities.

More important, economic sanctions often wreak havoc on innocent people and increase the power of the very leaders we despise. When applied broadside—as against North Korea, Cuba, Iran, and Iraq—economic sanctions mix the vices of carpet and neutron bombing. They hit hardest at the most vulnerable—the poor, the very young, the very old, and the sick. They leave unharmed, indeed strengthen, the real targets—political, military, and economic elites. Indeed, those in power relish adversity. Like Mussolini in 1935, they defiantly declare:

> At the League of Nations, they dared to speak of sanctions. To sanctions of an economic character we will reply with our discipline, with our sobriety, and with our spirit of sacrifice. To sanctions of a military character we will reply with orders of a military character.

Bombast is not the only benefit to those in power. They control the borders and thus profit from smuggling. They control the ration tickets and thus tighten their grip over the populace at large. It is one thing to sanction a semi-democratic country like South Africa, Pakistan, or Indonesia. In such cases, sanctions applied adroitly may be cited by domestic dissidents to alter internal policy. It is quite another matter to sanction a country ruled by Kim Il Sung, Castro, Saddam Hussein, or an Ayatollah.

Most important, secondary sanctions imposed by the United States against its allies and friends—the approach pioneered by Sen. Jesse Helms (R-N.C.), and Rep. Dan Burton (R-Ind.), refined by Sen. Alfonse D'Amato (R-N.Y.), and now emulated by dozens of state and municipal governments—furnish an international rallying flag against American hegemony. Americans above all should understand symbolic offenses. The British tea tax imposed no real economic hardship. It did inspire a revolution against the greatest power of the day.

## What Can Be Done?

The path out of America's folly is clear, but it will require decisive steps by the White House. Five steps are essential:

*First*, the United States should seldom impose sanctions when it cannot marshal support among its friends. To paraphrase Richard

Haass (of the Brookings Institution), this is a game for posses, not Lone Rangers. Ideally, the United Nations Security Council should support the sanctions. At a minimum, our NATO allies, or made-to-order posses in Latin America, Asia, or the Middle East, should endorse the effort.

*Second*, we should realize that sanctions typically have more value as carrots than as sticks. In other words, they are more useful when lifted than when imposed. This was recently illustrated by the U.S.-China summit agreement restraining Iran's delivery of missiles and nuclear materials to Iran in exchange for U.S. relaxation of nuclear technology controls. Another example is our complex and costly diplomacy with North Korea.

*Third*, as a corollary, the president must have unfettered freedom to lift sanctions step by step when he obtains appropriate cooperation from the target country. Sanctions legislation enacted by Congress, states, or municipalities should be vetoed, or challenged in court, when it does not contain a national interest waiver exercisable by the President.

*Fourth*, in the great majority of cases, sanctions should target elites, not the populace at large. Iraqis are not our enemy. Nor are Cubans. We can be imaginative in targeting elites. We can single out individuals and agencies that give offense or outrage. We can devise civil and criminal punishments so that their persons and property are at risk whenever they travel or do business in the civilized world.

*Fifth and finally*, broadside sanctions should be seen—by the White House, the State Department, and the Pentagon, as well as by the foreign target—as a prelude to force, not as a substitute for force. Powerless people do not deserve despicable governments, not in Iraq, not in Nigeria, not in Cuba. But unless we are prepared to remove bad governments with military force, we have no business heaping prolonged punishment on innocent people.

# 12. Caterpillar Inc.: A Case Study in America's CAT-astrophic Sanctions Policy

*William C. Lane*

To the staff and guests of the Cato Institute, on behalf of Caterpillar Inc., I would like to thank you for this opportunity to share our concerns about the proliferation of U.S. unilateral foreign policy sanctions and the importance of engagement. Caterpillar is proud to be the leader of the 676-member USA*ENGAGE effort. However, for today's purposes, I would like to restrict my comments to how Caterpillar has been affected by recent sanctions.

But before I do, let me say a few words about Cato. I know of no other organization that consistently recognizes the power of the marketplace or the positive impact that economic engagement has on societies than the Cato Institute. Cato will never be accused of being a summer soldier or sunshine "free trader." Nor will it be charged with compromising its principles to curry favor with a politically influential constituency. Caterpillar is proud to be a supporter of Cato.

But enough said about the virtues of Cato. Let me now talk about the virtues of another great organization. Caterpillar is headquartered in Peoria, Illinois; it is the world's leading producer of construction equipment and engines; and most important, it has been my employer for the past 23 years.

At Caterpillar, we believe we have special standing to discuss the issue of unilateral sanctions. As you may know, Caterpillar's business strategy is unique in that we compete globally from what is primarily a U.S. manufacturing base. As a result, we rank as one of America's largest exporters. But relying on a U.S. manufacturing

William C. Lane is the Washington director of governmental affairs for Caterpillar Inc.

base also means that when the United States imposes unilateral sanctions, the impact is greater on us than on many other companies.

Caterpillar also has a keen appreciation of the way unilateral sanctions undermined our competitiveness in the early 1980s as a result of the Soviet pipeline sanctions. You may recall that at that time Caterpillar was forced to cede the Soviet market to our Japanese competitors. As a result of that policy:

- 12,000 worker-years of work were transferred from Illinois to Japan.
- Caterpillar and other U.S. exporters were tainted as unreliable suppliers.
- Komatsu of Japan grew in strength, which allowed them to compete more effectively against Caterpillar on a global basis— a legacy that is still with us today.
- And the Soviets completed their pipeline ahead of schedule.

I might add that even though Russia now has a popularly elected government, our customers still ask if we can be counted on as a reliable supplier. Farmers from Central Illinois can recount similar stories about how the Soviet grain embargo hurt their businesses.

Getting one's arms around the problems associated with unilateral sanctions is a daunting project. We note that the President's Export Council reports that U.S. unilateral sanctions threaten 75 countries, or 52 percent of the world's population. Including recent sanctions against India, that number increases to two-thirds of the world's population. The National Association of Manufacturers documented more than 60 U.S. unilateral sanctions in just the past five years. Increasingly, the policies are having serious trade and foreign policy implications.

At Caterpillar, we believe to properly evaluate the impact of sanctions the issue must be analyzed from several perspectives.

### Lost Exports and Jobs

Clearly, the most obvious impact of U.S. unilateral sanctions is the impact they have on U.S. exports and American jobs. At Caterpillar, we can document exports lost as a result of numerous sanctions regimes. A few recent examples include the following:

*Colombia.* As a result of sanctions imposed in 1996 and 1997, Caterpillar lost several important contracts to sell mining equipment to

Colombia's coal industry. The reason: European competitors had access to competitive export financing, which was forbidden to American companies by the U.S. government.

*China.* White House efforts to discourage the export of American-made products to China's Three Gorges Dam have reduced Cat sales in Central China. Even though the world's largest construction project is progressing as scheduled, U.S. companies still do not have access to export financing. Consequently, American companies are at a competitive disadvantage vis-à-vis their foreign competitors.

*Iran.* As a result of U.S. export restrictions imposed against Iran in 1995, the entire Iranian market for construction equipment and engines was completely ceded to European manufacturers.

*Canada.* Fear of being entangled in U.S. extraterritorial sanctions prompted a Canadian Cat customer to buy diesel engines from Europe. Last year, the potential customer told a Caterpillar sales representative that "since the engines were being incorporated into products that might be sold in the Mideast, the best way to avoid problems is to buy German."

*Sudan.* Immediately after President Clinton's November 4, 1997, imposition of a trade and investment embargo, Komatsu of Japan took out newspaper ads in Khartoum announcing its new Sudan sales and support locations. Since then, Caterpillar has lost several important export contracts.

### U.S. Firms Tainted as Unreliable Suppliers

To determine the cost of unilateral sanctions, one must recognize that lost exports can also occur as a result of being labeled as an unreliable supplier. This is of particular concern for producers of capital equipment. After all, the purchaser of a Caterpillar bulldozer or an off-highway truck is making a decision that will last decades. Any uncertainty about our ability to provide long-term product support from the United States gives our European and Japanese competitors a significant competitive advantage. Currently, the issue of being a reliable supplier is a major hurdle we must overcome in our efforts to sell in Russia, Malaysia, and several Republics of the former Soviet Union.

### Enhanced Competitiveness of Foreign Rivals

Even though it is hard to quantify, it is important to recognize that U.S. unilateral sanctions can enhance the competitiveness of our foreign competitors. When the U.S. cedes an export market to its foreign competitors, it has in effect provided them with a protected "home market." As a result, they not only benefit from increased economies of scale but have the opportunity to cross-subsidize sales in other markets.

Put another way, when the U.S. government gave the Soviet market to Komatsu, Caterpillar also ended up with a more formidable competitor in Europe, Asia, and the Western Hemisphere.

## Sanctions Undermine Other U.S. Objectives

Perhaps the biggest cost of sanctions is the way they affect other U.S. foreign policy goals. We note with concern that, at a time when we are trying to maintain multilateral support for a united policy toward Iraq, we find that the United States has imposed or threatened sanctions against all Arab members of the Gulf War alliance—except Kuwait—and three of four other permanent members of the U.N. Security Council. One need not be a foreign policy expert to realize that these sanctions may be one of the reasons why it has been so hard to win an agreement on a multilateral sanctions policy toward Iraq.

In Asia, at a time when the International Monetary Fund is working diligently to stabilize the financial crisis there—which directly affects the entire U.S. economy—the United States is maintaining sanctions against South Korea over the issue of worker rights and threatening sanctions against Malaysia. In addition, several U.S. state and local governments are further complicating U.S. foreign policy by targeting sanctions against Indonesia.

There is also a cost when U.S. sanctions violate our trade and treaty obligations. When that situation occurs, we undermine the very multilateral institutions that can play an important role not only by enhancing the world economy but also in promoting positive change. For example, if extraterritorial sanctions violate U.S. commitments made to the World Trade Organization, the United States has less leverage to force other countries to honor their obligations under the General Agreement on Tariffs and Trade. As a result, the World Trade Organization loses credibility and Americans do not fully benefit from a more open trading system.

Allow me to conclude by emphasizing that Caterpillar fully recognizes that much of the world remains a dangerous place. We realize that, at times, sanctions—even unilateral ones—may be necessary.

If that appears to be the case, we believe that unilateral sanctions should be considered only after Congress and the Executive branch have exhausted potential alternatives such as diplomatic initiatives and multilateral pressure. If unilateral sanctions must be considered, they should be judged by (1) their likelihood of actually achieving their intended results; (2) the harm they will cause to other national interests; and (3) the costs imposed on Americans. Finally, we believe future unilateral sanctions should be subject to a meaningful accountability review every two years.

At this time I should emphasize that Caterpillar, like the Cato Institute, is unapologetic in its belief that engagement can be a powerful force for positive change when pursued at all levels—political, diplomatic, economic, charitable, religious, educational, and cultural. In contrast, a unilateral sanction can isolate the United States—taking away the influence and credibility we gain by being involved. It is time that the United States treated the issue of unilateral sanctions in a more serious and deliberative manner.

PART V

HUMAN RIGHTS AND CIVIL LIBERTIES

# 13. Free Trade and Human Rights: The Moral Case for Engagement

*Robert A. Sirico*

The policy community has been debating an interesting question: whether, or to what extent, concerns about human rights and the right to free religious expression should affect U.S. trade relations with countries. That issue is also directly connected with competing visions of the nature of trade relations themselves. Do they consist solely of businesses and consumers reaping gains from exchange across borders? Or should those exchanges be managed by government regulations and subsidized by international lending institutions?

Pope John Paul II, in his speech to the Vatican Diplomatic Corps in 1995, had the following to say:

> In today's interdependent world, a whole network of exchanges is forcing nations to live together, whether they like it or not. But there is a need to pass from simply living together to partnership. Isolation is no longer appropriate. The embargo in particular, clearly defined by law, is an instrument that needs to be used with great discernment, and it must be subjected to strict legal and ethical criteria. It is a means of exerting pressure on governments which have violated the international code of good conduct and of causing them to reconsider their choices. But in a sense it is also an act of force and, as certain cases of the present moment demonstrate, it inflicts grave hardships upon the people of the countries at which it is aimed. . . . Before imposing such measures, it is always imperative to foresee the humanitarian consequences of sanctions, without failing to respect the just proportion that such measures should have in relation to the very evil which they are meant to remedy.

Father Robert A. Sirico, a Catholic priest, is cofounder and president of the Acton Institute for the Study of Religion and Liberty, based in Grand Rapids, Mich.

The recent case of India illustrates the confusion that clouds the issue. The Indian government's testing in May 1998 of nuclear devices in blatant disregard of the Nuclear Proliferation Prevention Act enacted by the U.S. Congress in 1994 raises a human rights issue because controlling the spread of nuclear weapons is important to the safety and security of us all.

In response to those tests, the United States imposed economic sanctions. But let us look at the fine print. Aaron Lukas of the Cato Institute pointed out in the *Journal of Commerce* on May 22, 1998, that the "sanctions" are largely an end to wasteful foreign aid and corporate welfare spending. Between 1946 and 1996, India received some $50 billion from Washington. The sanctions have ended that flow of government-to-government aid. The sanctions also block Export-Import Bank and Overseas Private Investment Corporation loans that directly subsidized private trade and investment. Those programs actually impeded economic progress by channeling resources in ways the market would not otherwise allocate them.

Those are the kinds of so-called sanctions any believer in free trade should be glad to accept. Yet the sanctions also prohibit U.S. banks from lending to state-owned Indian enterprises and ban millions of dollars in exports, something that is difficult to justify. That is an example of U.S. involvement in the micromanagement of international trade with no expectation that the sanctions will actually achieve their goal.

I cite the case of India because it shows the muddy thinking that dominates this debate. The first error is to confuse aid with trade. The second error, evident within some sectors of the business community, is to dismiss the issue of human rights and to remain silent, as individuals and as a nation, in the face of human rights abuses in the belief that economic interests ought to prevail in foreign relations. A third error—currently promoted by a diminishing segment of the Christian right—is to politicize international trade by making it an arena for human rights battles.

## Trade Yes, Aid No

The debate on U.S.–Chinese trade relations, in particular, has led to vigorous disagreement between some conservative Christian activists and advocates of free trade. This becomes most visible during the annual debate on renewing China's "most favored nation" status (which means, in today's political context, normal trade relations). The implications are broader, however, because many nations restrict the freedom of religious practice. In particular, Russia has extended full freedom of worship to only four main religions while delegitimizing others. Cuba only recently began to tolerate public expressions of the Christian faith.

Since the great China debate, dozens of bills that would make trade relations contingent on the protection of human rights have been introduced in Congress. Included on the list of currently targeted countries are Burma, China, Colombia, Cuba, India, Indonesia, Iran, Iraq, Libya, Mauritania, Mexico, Nigeria, North Korea, Pakistan, Peru, Russia, Serbia, Sudan, Syria, Thailand, Trinidad and Tobago, Turkey, and Zaire. The United States has imposed sanctions more than 60 times in the past five years—more than half the total of all sanctions imposed since World War II.

Then there is the Godzilla of all sanctions bills, the Wolf-Specter bill, which the House passed overwhelmingly in May 1998. It would have empowered the State Department to classify countries on the basis of perceived oppression of religious groups, with a finding of wrongdoing leading to an automatic imposition of targeted sanctions. Some of the sanctions, as well as other parts of the original bill, were cut. The final version that passed Congress focuses on cutting off foreign aid or limiting the granting of visas, and its trade sanctions were dropped.

Without regard to this specific piece of legislation, one is still left to wonder if the changes reflect a change of heart regarding the effects of the sanctions themselves or whether they are only a bow to political reality. I believe that many people who support the bill view it as a first step in a global social engineering project in which the United States becomes the world's moral arbiter. If so, the bill can only lead to worse legislation that will eventually be counterproductive to the cause of open societies, religious freedom, and international cooperation.

The House version contained extreme sanctions against Sudan. Is that the direction in which the bill's supporters would like to see U.S. policy go in the future? Is the bill only a wedge for more extreme measures to come? We must keep our eye on its trajectory.

The reasons cited for the imposition of sanctions on countries mentioned are various, but most relate to human rights. I believe that what activists say about those countries is true; should we then trade with regimes that restrict religious freedom and violate human rights?

People on all sides of the issue agree on certain goals: we want tyranny to end wherever it exists, and in its place we want to see the establishment of free societies that will ensure the dignity of human life and protect freedom of conscience and religion.

Some vocal Christian activists emphasize only human rights. On the basis of extensive documentation of torture; political imprisonment; religious persecution; mandatory abortions; suppression of churches; jailing of priests, bishops, and evangelists; and even murder, those activists have compared the present situation in China and elsewhere with Nazi Germany and the Soviet Union.

In light of those realities, many well-intentioned believers call for a curtailment of trade relations, and some even call for a complete trade embargo, drawing a comparison with our past relations with Nazis and communists. That is not a valid comparison, since our dealings with Nazis involved fighting a bloody world war and engaging in aerial bombings of German cities. Our dealings with the Soviet Union involved the relentless production of weapons of mass destruction and a huge and expensive military buildup.

**The Chinese Economic Miracle**

The pro–free-trade business interests emphasize different points, and suggest a different agenda. They point out that China is experiencing a historic economic boom which was brought about by a rapid transition, beginning 15 years ago, from centrally planned socialism to an increasingly capitalist system organized along federalist lines.

Supporters of free enterprise also have observed that, though the Chinese leaders still maintain that China is a communist state, they have, in fact, completely redefined the term. Tax rates have been slashed (and in some regions are actually lower than those of the United States), industries have been privatized, labor markets have been freed in relative terms, housing ownership is encouraged and growing, and joint ventures with Western companies are increasing rapidly.

The Chinese stock market invites wide public participation, while industrialism and technological progress are proceeding at a breakneck pace, especially in the south. With more shipping lanes opening

106

up each month, China has begun to share in the boom as well. The results have been astounding: in one generation, China has moved from total domination by one of the world's most murderous regimes to one of increased material prosperity, freedom of movement, rising commercial opportunity, and relative abundance.

Proponents of free enterprise also point out that the United States has benefited from Chinese economic growth. As a result of our trade relations with China, American consumers enjoy high-quality consumer goods of all types, from high-tech products to clothing. Browse any U.S. shopping center and you will find picture frames, calculators, napkins and napkin holders, glassware, party favors, containers, kitchen appliances, toys, puzzles, shoes, paper products, electric fans, cosmetics—to name a few items—all featuring the "Made in China" label. American consumers have access to those items at low prices, and the import boom has freed capital and labor in this country to concentrate on producing items in which we have a comparative advantage as a nation: financial services, computers, software, agricultural goods, detergents, tires, vehicles of all sorts, furniture, building supplies, and many other things that are available for export to China and other nations.

Moreover, one can no longer say that many classes of goods are made solely in one country. Computers can feature American microchips and software, Japanese communications packages, and Chinese electronic parts. The same is true of cars, clothing, and foodstuffs. The recently announced merger of Daimler-Benz and Chrysler is a case in point. What will happen to the "buy America" campaign with respect to the new cars produced by a German-American company? All of those products provide good examples of ways trade can benefit people of all societies.

### Business Turns a Blind Eye

The Christian right and supporters of free enterprise view the present situation in radically different ways. What strikes me, however, is the way each side seems unable to concede that the other side can contribute a fuller understanding of present realities.

In many cases, those in favor of free enterprise have turned a blind eye to human rights abuses for fear that mentioning them might endanger the growth and expansion of trade. They frequently exhibit little concern about religious persecution and tend to regard human rights activists and religious leaders as belligerents or idealists who do not understand the "real" world.

The same is true of government leaders. In particular, the Clinton administration's dealings with China have been characterized by a moral blindness to the reality of suffering and persecution in China. Jimmy Carter, writing in the *New York Times* last year, exhibited the same myopia. That is hardly a new phenomenon. U.S. government officials in the Roosevelt, Truman, Nixon, and Carter administrations befriended Stalin, Khrushchev, and Brezhnev, hoping to win their favor, but showing little concern for the millions who suffered under their rule. Truly, the American corporate lobby is capable of deep cynicism and disregard for the basic freedoms of the mass of people living under authoritarian regimes.

Worse, rather than trade on a purely commercial basis, many corporate interests seek special privileges and subsidies. Those include loans from the Export-Import Bank, which underwrites foreign investments at taxpayer expense, and investment guarantees from the Overseas Private Investment Corporation, which also operates at taxpayer expense. They have lobbied for World Bank infrastructure development loans, support from the International Monetary Fund, subsidies from the United Nations and its myriad affiliates, and much more.

To them, free trade is bound up with such guarantees. The business lobbies that work hard against economic sanctions rarely mention those extra perks, or if they do speak about them, they support them. Foreign aid, loan guarantees, and subsidies are not free trade but the opposite: government planning. Such subsidized investment comes at the expense of the American people, who are ultimately responsible for those loans and guarantees. It is the height of naiveté for American business to believe that the government should intervene in the trade process on their behalf but that political intervention will not backfire against their interests.

For any true free trader, such tax-funded interventions and distortions are anathema. I support the immediate cutoff of all IMF loans and the abolition of all government programs that subsidize foreign trade, beginning with regimes that engage in political and religious persecution, but certainly not limited to them.

Fortunately, such loans and aid are not what sustains the international economy. Most of our trade with the world is not subsidized;

it reflects the common interests of manufacturers, consumers, ship-pers, entrepreneurs, and bankers in all countries. By all means, cut off privileges and subsidies, but do not damage the genuine commercial relations that have so improved the lives of people around the world.

## Economics 101 for Christians

I have discussed the selective vision and moral blindness of certain business interests. Now, I will address the economic misunderstand-ings of conservative Christian activists. Trading with a country is not the same thing as placing a moral imprimatur on the government of that country. Some Christian activists have demonstrated an embarrassing lack of understanding of that basic fact.

To say, "I support trade sanctions on country X," really means, "I think that American consumers ought to be punished by higher taxes for their desire to buy products from country X. American producers ought to be forced by their own government to invest someplace where they are less likely to make money. The U.S. gov-ernment, not markets, ought to determine where and what people buy and sell across borders with their own money. Moreover, the people in country X ought to be denied essential goods and services and the right to enjoy the fruits of the international division of labor."

Let us be honest about the economic consequences of sanctions, although passionate advocates of sanctions evidently do not think much about economics. For instance, in the debate about trade with China, not once have I seen any discussion in their writings about the Chinese economic miracle and what it means to the people of China, including the Christian church in China. Not once have I seen an acknowledgment that the Chinese government has allowed an unprecedented increase in the freedom to own property, to work, to engage in enterprise, to pursue economic interest, to own a home, to build a business, and to keep profits.

Indeed, in the writings of conservative Christian activists, the words "profit" and "economic interest" have been used as if they were the devil's own words. One expects such anti-business rhetoric from the left, but it is disconcerting when it comes from conserva-tives. Not once have I heard discussed what the explosive growth in material prosperity and the new freedoms that have made it possible mean for China's future. Every day, we hear more news of

China's path to reform. In a few years, for example, more than half its state-run industries will be in private hands.

How can we act as if China is one huge prison camp, when the far more complex reality is there for anyone to see? Members of the American business community who frequently deal with China—among them Christians who devote their lives to serving others through economic endeavors—are dismayed at what is being written and said by some conservative Christians involved in the debate. An economic miracle is taking place—an historic chance that the Chinese people will be made permanently free to pursue their individual dreams—and yet all some people can talk about is thumbscrews and prison bars. Like socialists of old, they have even taken to disparaging economics itself.

That is a huge error. Sanctions against Cuba have done little to encourage freedom of expression there. But the influx of outside influence that came with the pope's visit in January 1998 did succeed in opening up Cuban society somewhat. I was fortunate enough to be there during that time. Not once did I hear an average Cuban, struggling to make ends meet under extraordinarily difficult circumstances, call for the extension of U.S. sanctions, a good indication of how unsuccessful sanctions have been.

Most of the countries likely to be hit by the Wolf-Specter bill on religious persecution are prime markets for future exports. But the export of goods also means the export of influence, both on the people and on the regimes in question. We should not embrace bills that would limit our influence; we should embrace strategies that strengthen our influence, while at the same time fostering the development of private networks that can circumvent official channels.

### Handmaidens of Protection

In addition, advocates of sanctions seem unaware of the role they unwittingly play in the protectionist cause. Leaders of some industries in this country would like to use the power of the U.S. government to gain an unfair advantage in trade. They are protectionists who seek profits, not by serving the consumer, but by shutting others out of the market with import quotas, tariffs, and lawsuits against importers. Since the Industrial Revolution, protectionists have brought about high prices, economic inefficiencies, recessions, depressions, and wars, all of which consolidate the central power of the state.

Protectionist interests sell out free enterprise principles and seek special protection from the government at the expense of consumers. Keeping the protectionists at bay has always been a high priority of all believers in human liberty and human rights.

Whether they know it or not, conservative religious activists who call for trade sanctions and favor cutting off commerce with foreign nations are playing directly into the hands of the protectionist lobbies. They are tools of the worst of the American corporate class— a class that enriches itself at everyone else's expense. Protectionism and sanctions are not only bad economics, they are also the politics of business and corporate corruption.

## Conclusion

Christians are right to pray for persecuted people around the world. We are right to engage in civic activism. We are right to send missionaries to serve their needs. Indeed, during the cold war, Christians, together with human rights activists, exerted pressure in every way they knew. And though many of the captive nations are now free, and religious toleration has arrived in many former communist states where evangelization is under way, persecution still persists in practically every country where the government continues to operate in an authoritarian and totalitarian manner.

It is time for both sides to concede that their opponents have some valid arguments. I see no advantage for either side in denying the reality of human rights abuses or in pretending that embargoes and trade wars have any constructive role to play in ending them. There is no moral justification for withholding vigorous protest of inhumane policies because they may threaten commercial relations, but neither will anything be gained by linking free trade with accommodation to Hitler. When we speak about our trade relations with foreign countries, I see no reason why we cannot do it with both moral passion and economic understanding.

There is room for consensus on the question of how trade policy and human rights policy intersect, but it is going to require some give and take on both sides. We can start with multinational business dropping its support for tax-subsidized trade programs, and with human rights activists trying to understand the role of business, and

111

especially the role of free trade, in enhancing the material well-being of all people and the promotion of human rights.

In conclusion, Ronald Reagan's words are worth recalling: "The freer the flow of world trade, the stronger the tides of human progress and peace among nations."

# 14. The Costs of Encryption Export Controls: What about Our Constitutional Values?

*Kenneth C. Bass III*

Those who have followed the continuing debate over the wisdom of export controls on cryptographic software are well acquainted with the arguments. Industry contends that export controls simply hinder American software developers and have, in effect, created a viable niche for foreign software companies.

The argument is basically one of economic security. Because there is an increasing demand for robust security for electronic commerce and other Internet transactions, someone will fulfill the demand. If American companies cannot build on their substantial advantages, foreign companies will seize the moment to dominate the market. The other alternative we are now seeing is the trend among American companies to go offshore for their strong encryption development. Unilateral U.S. controls, so the argument goes, are ineffective in preventing the spread of strong encryption and inherently impair traditional American strength in developing and marketing applications software.

On the other side, the government argues that widespread deployment of strong encryption will hinder law enforcement and—at least in theory—national security interests. To these advocates the loss of economic advantage is more than offset by the, admittedly temporary, benefit of prolonging the government's ability to gather telecommunications information through electronic surveillance.

The facts seem to support both sides. Yes, export controls effectively export jobs from the United States to other countries. And yes, widespread deployment of strong encryption would hinder law enforcement and intelligence collection efforts. The problem with the

Kenneth C. Bass III is a partner at Venable, Baetjer, Howard & Civiletti.

debate is that it is seemingly irreconcilable. There is no "marketplace mechanism" in which the *software and law enforcement* communities can compete to see which side the American people really support. Instead we are left with an apparently paralyzed Congress that debates the issues, continues to pray for a "technological solution," and in the meantime simply contributes to the stalemate by continued inaction.

Years ago some of us tried to persuade the government advocates that the eventual spread of strong encryption was inevitable and that national security interests would be better served by trying to facilitate domination of the encryption market by American—rather than foreign—companies. That effort has failed. The Administration continues to believe that government controls serve the national interest.

While the public debate on the Hill has focused on the conflict between economic security and traditional national security values, a simultaneous debate is moving along in the judicial branch that pits the national security concerns against other values. That other debate does not raise issues of economics, but instead raises arguments that encryption export controls conflict with fundamental constitutional values.

Three cases are now pending in federal courts that challenge the export control structure as it relates to cryptography. Philip Karn, a software engineer with Qualcomm, a California-based communications technology company, filed the first such Karn litigation in Washington. Karn sought and was granted permission to export copies of Bruce Schneier's essential guidebook on computerized cryptography, *Applied Cryptography*. Recognizing that any effort to block a book would pose a direct challenge to fundamental First Amendment values, the government concluded that the book itself could be exported. But then Executive Branch agencies went further and ruled that a copy of portions of the book *in text file form* on a floppy diskette could not be exported.

The government justified the apparent inconsistency as an effort to regulate a machine and not an effort to regulate speech. The diskette in issue contains the source code listings of several cryptographic algorithms, source code that is printed as part of the appendix in the book. The government argues that source code on a diskette, unlike source code in a book, can be "readily converted" into an operating encryption program, the export of which might harm national security interests.

In the complaint I filed on Karn's behalf, we challenge the agency action on two separate constitutional grounds. We contend primarily that the distinction between source code text in a printed book and the identical material in digital form on magnetic media is irrational, arbitrary, capricious, and a violation of substantive due process. We also contend that inasmuch as source code is written by computer programmers to communicate ideas and techniques to other pro-grammers, it is a form of "pure speech" that is entitled to the same First Amendment protections that resulted in the decision not to regulate the book.

Essentially the same First Amendment claim has been raised by two professors in separate suits, one filed in California and the other in Ohio. In each case, the plaintiff seeks to distribute cryptographic source code as part of teaching activities, again, an activity tradition-ally protected by the First Amendment.

The *Karn* case and the California case have each resulted in initial decisions at the trial court level. In *Karn* the late Judge Charles Richey dismissed our First Amendment claim, holding that the govern-ment's purpose in preventing the export of the diskette was not to suppress speech but to regulate conduct. He therefore invoked the balancing test used in "communicative conduct" cases and con-cluded that the government's interest weighed heavier on the scales.

The California case produces an opposite result. There Judge Marylyn Patel concluded that computer source code is indeed a form of speech fully protected by the First Amendment and rejected the existing export control regime as an impermissible form of prior restraint.

Both cases were appealed. Shortly before the *Karn* case was argued, President Clinton transferred responsibility for administering export controls on cryptography from the State Department to the Depart-ment of Commerce. That transfer produced the not-unexpected appellate decision to remand the case for further consideration in light of new statutory issues raised by the transfer of responsibility. That case now is back before the trial court, where Judge Louis Oberdorfer will rule on the additional issues not considered by Judge Richey.

The government's appeal in the California case was argued before the Ninth Circuit Court of Appeals early in December 1997. A decision has not been rendered. The third case remains in the trial court where a motion for summary judgment was recently argued.

Each of the lawsuits raises First Amendment arguments on behalf of individuals who wish to communicate cryptographic source code to others. But the constitutional values implicated by the continued controls on export of cryptographic software extend beyond those claims. Government efforts to delay the inevitable spread of strong cryptography necessarily affect the First Amendment rights of ordinary citizens, not just software engineers and professors. Cryptography is an important tool of communications in the modern world. The dramatic explosion in Internet activity means that many Americans—as well as non-Americans—now use e-mail over the Internet as a means of communicating with family, friends, and business associates around the world. Those communications are plainly speech, entitled to First Amendment protections. To the extent that widespread deployment of strong encryption would contribute to an increased sense of security in using the Internet, private speech through electronic channels would expand.

Government regulation of cryptography thus affects individual First Amendment freedoms because cryptography in the modern world is itself a tool of speech. Indeed, for those who would choose to communicate ideas that are threats to the nondemocratic government that rules in their country, cryptography may be an essential tool of speech.

Freedom of speech is not the only constitutional value threatened by government regulation of cryptography. Encryption enables people to keep their communications private and avoid disclosing personal information to the government or uninvited other parties. As such, cryptography enhances personal privacy, a value that has found protection in the penumbra—if not the specific language—of the Constitution.

The general public has not yet perceived the issues of speech and privacy that are affected by current controls on cryptography. The public may not perceive that threat until and unless the FBI succeeds in its quest for imposition of controls on domestic use of cryptography. But by then it will be too late. We will have lost some of the freedom we now enjoy and to that extent our constitutional rights will have been diminished.

The trumpet call for citizen concern over threatened loss of constitutional freedoms has yet to be heard. It may well be that the mystery and lack of familiarity that surround the cryptographic sciences limit our ability to make this debate an issue of general public concern. But unless the public is aroused to see the threat to our individual freedoms that lies beneath the surface of today's debate, we are likely to see a continued legislative stalemate and prolongation of controls, with all of their attendant costs—economic as well as intangible.

# Index

# Cato Institute

Founded in 1977, the Cato Institute is a public policy research foundation dedicated to broadening the parameters of policy debate to allow consideration of more options that are consistent with the traditional American principles of limited government, individual liberty, and peace. To that end, the Institute strives to achieve greater involvement of the intelligent, concerned lay public in questions of policy and the proper role of government.

The Institute is named for *Cato's Letters,* libertarian pamphlets that were widely read in the American Colonies in the early 18th century and played a major role in laying the philosophical foundation for the American Revolution.

Despite the achievement of the nation's Founders, today virtually no aspect of life is free from government encroachment. A pervasive intolerance for individual rights is shown by government's arbitrary intrusions into private economic transactions and its disregard for civil liberties.

To counter that trend, the Cato Institute undertakes an extensive publications program that addresses the complete spectrum of policy issues. Books, monographs, and shorter studies are commissioned to examine the federal budget, Social Security, regulation, military spending, international trade, and myriad other issues. Major policy conferences are held throughout the year, from which papers are published thrice yearly in the *Cato Journal.* The Institute also publishes the quarterly magazine *Regulation.*

In order to maintain its independence, the Cato Institute accepts no government funding. Contributions are received from foundations, corporations, and individuals, and other revenue is generated from the sale of publications. The Institute is a nonprofit, tax-exempt, educational foundation under Section 501(c)3 of the Internal Revenue Code.

CATO INSTITUTE
1000 Massachusetts Ave., N.W.
Washington, D.C. 20001